ETHNIC CHRONOLOGY SERIES
NUMBER 21

# The Lithuanians in America 1651-1975

## A Chronology & Fact Book

Compiled and edited by
**Algirdas M. Budreckis**

**1976**
OCEANA PUBLICATIONS, INC.
DOBBS FERRY, NEW YORK

Library of Congress Catalog Card No. 76-6680
ISBN 0-379-00517-4



Manufactured in the United States of America

## TABLE OF CONTENTS

## EDITOR'S FOREWORD

Immigrants from the southeastern shores of the Baltic, from Lithuania, settled in North America as far back as the first half of the seventeenth century. Often confused with Slavic or Germanic peoples, the Lithuanians as an ethnic group have contributed to the settlement and development of the United States. Yet very little is known about them or their accomplishments, despite the fact that over one million six hundred thousand Americans can claim Lithuanian ancestry. One reason for this dirth of information in English is the inherent reticence of this ethnic group. Very few non-Lithuanians are aware of the fact that Chicago has a Lithuanian-speaking population that ranks second only to Vilnius, the capital of Lithuania. Few Americans realize that there are over half a million citizens in Pennsylvania who are of Lithuanian stock. On the whole, Lithuanians tend to be modest. Until recently, very little systematic study has been conducted concerning the work and accomplishments of their forebearers in this country. These circumstances, in part, account for the few studies, books or pamphlets on the cultural, social and civic activities of the Lithuanian-American community in the English language.

The present study is an attempt to introduce the non-Lithuanian reader to the varied and variegated historical experience of the Lithuanians in America. Many of the events and the major portion of documents quoted are rendered into English for the first time.

Lithuanian immigration to these shores has gone through several periods or waves. Each wave of immigrants was distinct in its motivation to come to America; its social composition varies from period to period. Thus, the first Lithuanian settlers were nobles, soldiers of fortune, artisans and would-be scholars, protestant in religion. They left the religious and national strife of mid-seventeenth century Lithuania to settle down in the tolerant Dutch and English colonies on the Atlantic shore. Most of these early colonists married into Anglo-Saxon families and in a generation lost their Baltic heritage. The second wave consisted of militant gentry or noblemen, who had flocked to the American revolutionary cause. They were influenced by the French Enlightenment and, like their Polish colleagues, had fought unsuccessfully to rid their homeland of the encroachments of the Russians. Some of these volunteer Lithuanian soldiers, like Miklasevicius, found a permanent home in the United States.

The failure of the 1831 Rebellion in Poland and Lithuania against Russian rule again brought several hundred Lithuanian nobles, former soldiers and even patriotic clergymen to the United States. These newcomers were political emigres, devoted for the most part to the ideals of the old Polish-Lithuanian Commonwealth.

The fourth wave, spanning a period of nearly fifty years (1868-1914) saw the arrival of five hundred thousand Lithuanian immigrants. Though peasants for the most part, these newcomers differed from the second and third waves in the fact that they were not of a pro-Polish orientation. They were influenced by the

Lithuanian National Renaissance and devoted much of their energy and resources to establish newspapers and cultural societies. This immigration provided American industry with physical resources. Countless thousands of able-bodied Lithuanian peasants labored on the railway construction projects, in the coal mines, the slaughterhouses, and the iron and steel mills and foundries. They also founded numerous churches, cultural and civic homes, newspapers and book publishing houses.

The fifth wave came in the inter-war years (1919-1940). Though small in absolute numbers (30,000), this group provided intellectuals and cultural leaders for the old colonies of compatriots.

The sixth and most recent wave consists of the so-called displaced persons (1949-1953). The displaced persons were political refugees from Communist domination. They were intellectuals, cultural leaders and professionals. They and their children are to be found among skilled workers, physicians, engineers, chemists and businessmen. Their children are on university faculties, in all branches of the arts and sciences. They are also responsible for the renewed interest in Lithuanian culture and heritage.

The chronology and concomitant documents will outline the three hundred year history of the Lithuanians in America. The reader will note varied levels and forms of expression that this ethnic group has devoted its energies to. Like all outlines, this study is incomplete. The diversification of organizations and activities will only bear out the fact that the Lithuanians, like other ethnically-conscious communities, are dynamic and complex.

Algirdas M. Budreckis
Boston, Massachusetts

1651 Governor Peter Stuyvesant of the Dutch colony of New Amsterdam razed the Swedish fort of Nassau and named it Fort Kasimier, probably to irritate the Swedes warring against the Poles and Lithuanians. Another reason for the name was the fact that there were Polish and Lithuanian soldiers of fortune in the Dutch military expedition. The Swedes regained the fort in 1654 and named it Fort Trinity. The following year it was named Nieuw Amstel by the returning Dutch, and New Castle, Delaware, when the British conquered New Netherlands.

1659 On April 10th, acting upon the request of the Burgomasters of New Amsterdam to furnish a teacher of the classics for the colony's adolescents, the Directors of the West India Company at Amsterdam engaged as Latin schoolmaster in New Amsterdam one Dr. Alexander Carolus Cursius (Kursius). They advised Governor Stuyvesant, by a letter dated April 25th: "How much trouble we have taken to find a Latin schoolmaster is shown by the fact, that now one Alexander Carolus Cursius, late professor in Lithuania, goes over." Dr. Cursius taught school in New Amsterdam for two years, from 1659 to 1661. He is credited with being the first secondary teacher in America.

When the English from New England began to settle upstate New York, Governor Stuyvesant appealed to his directors in Holland, in a letter dated September 4, 1659: "To cause that some homeless Polish, Lithuanian, Prussian, Jutlandish or Flemish farmers (who, as we trust, are soon and easily to be found during this eastern and northern war) may be sent over by the first ships."

1662 A number of Lithuanian protestants who had fled upheavals at home during the 1660s migrated to the Dutch colony of New Amsterdam. Others moved from Holland to England, from whence their services as craftsmen in the lumber industry were solicited in the New World. Settling in the English colonies they married local Anglo-Saxon women. Most of them assimilated, yet retained Lithuanian names: Butwill, Ardwill, Cantwill, Purvis.

1690 A group of Mennonites from Lithuania settled outside of Philadelphia, Pennsylvania, together with their co-religionists from Switzerland.

1777 Thaddeus Kosciuszko came to America, served in the Continental Corps of Artillery and Engineers. He fortified West Point and raised the idea of an American military academy. In the case of Tadas Kosciuska or, if you prefer Thaddeus Kosciuszko, Poles and Lithuanians have come to blows claiming him as their own. In truth he came from a Lithuanian noble family that received its nobility patent in the 15th century. Kosciuszko was born in a border region of the Grand Duchy of Lithuania. He spoke and wrote in Polish, and led the heroic Revolt of 1794 for the Polish-Lithuanian Commonwealth. On a number of occasions he wrote that he was a "Lithuanian of Poland."

The Continental Congress named Kosciuszko brigadier general of the Continental Army, in appreciation of his services as a colonel of engineers. Furthermore, he gained recognition as "the Father of American artillery" by reason of his authorship of the first American artillery manual "Manoevers of Horse Artillery," originally written in French and published in English translation by Colonel Jonathan Williams, Commandant of West Point Academy in 1808. This manual was reprinted in 1812 and became the standard text of American students of artillery problems.

There was at least one known Lithuanian noble who fought in the British Army. He was Count Grabouski (Grabauskas) who died a heroic death when the British stormed Fort Clinton, New York.

1777-1779 The following Lithuanians served in the Polish Legion of Count Casimir Pulaski, father of American cavalry: Joseph Gabriel, Captain Joseph Baldesque-Baldique, Count Katskootski, Captain Matthias Ragouski, and John de Zielinski. The last named died of wounds in 1779 received before Charleston. The Polonized Slovak noble, Maurice Bieniowski, who owned estates in Lithuania, also served under the Pole C. Pulaski.

1780 Captain John Quirin Meszkowski (Meskauskas) and Lieutenant Michael Grabowski (Grabauskas) saw action with Armand Louis de Gontaut Biron, duc de Lauzun's French Foreign Marine Legion, which fought on the American side in Connecticut, New York and the siege of Yorktown.

1782 On September 5th, the Continental Congress granted Feliks Milaszevicz of Boston the right to use his ship Scotch Trick in privateering operations against British shipping.

1783 On March 18th the Council of the Massachusetts Bay commissioned Miklaszevicz to use his schooner Prince Radvil in privateering operations against the British.

1793 In July, Louis Chodkiewicz, escutcheon of the Lithuanian noble family of Boreika-Katkevicius, married Ann Beekman in New York. Louis Chodkiewicz was recorded as a former Revolutionary War veteran.

Peter Kluge (1768-1849), a Lithuanian of Gumbine, East Prussia, worked as a Moravian missionary in the White River region of Indiana.

1795 On March 18th, Bishop John Carrol ordained Demetrius Augustine Gallitzin, descendent of the Lithuanian dynasty of Gediminas, as the first Roman Catholic Priest to have completed his theological studies and to have taken his vows in the United States. Known as "the Apostle of the Alleghenies," Rev. Gallitzin founded the town of Loretto, Pennsylvania. He was the first American priest to have written apologetic and polemical works in this country, viz.: "Defense of Catholic Principles" (1816).

1797 On August 19, Kosciuszko and his Lithuanian Secretary Julian Ursyn Niemcevicius arrived in Philadelphia. Because of Yellow Fever in the city, they went to General Anthony Walton White in New Brunswick, New Jersey. Afterwards they sojourned in Elizabeth. Kosciuszko proceeded to New York, where he was granted 500 acres by the United States Government for his past services. The next year Kosciuszko left for France where he served as liaison between his friend Thomas Jefferson and the leaders of Revolutionary France.

Julian Niemcevicius remained longer. He visited President Washington at Mount Vernon. In 1800 he married Colonel Kean's widow Susan Livingston of Elizabeth, New Jersey. From 1797 to 1802 he kept a diary in Polish containing much material about Elizabeth and his impressions of America.

1812-1815 The following Lithuanians served on the American side during the War of 1812: Corporal Jonas Bogas of the Kentucky Volunteer Cavalry Regiment, the Revolutionary War veteran Joseph Gabrielius (who was wounded defending Baltimore), John Kaska of the Kentucky militia, John Malus of the Kentucky 1st Cavalry Regiment, and George Zobiskie of the Norfolk, Virginia, Second Militia.

1832 In 1831 the Poles and Lithuanians staged an unsuccessful patriotic revolt against the Russians. Following the Revolt, many young Lithuanian and Polish nobles fled abroad. Among the insurrectionists who fled was Major Joseph Hordynski of the 10th Regiment of Lithuanian Lancers, attached to the Corps of General

Gelgaudas-Gielgud. Hordynski migrated to England and, with the aid of Samuel Gridley Howe of Boston, came to the United States in 1832. Here he published his book, "The History of the Late Polish Revolution", reprinted at Boston in four volumes in 1832 and 1833. Hordynski's book gave a first-hand account of the revolt in Lithuania. For an introduction Hordynski summarized Leon Chodzka's brief history of Lithuania. Therefore, Hordynski should be credited with writing the first history of Lithuania in America. He used the royalties of his book to purchase pistols and a sword and to attempt to return to the homeland. He was captured at the Austrian-Russian border and deported to Siberia as a rebel.

Another rebel Captain Alexander Bielaski-Beleckis arrived in Portland, Maine. From July 17, 1842 until 1850 he worked for the United States Land Office. Captain Bielaski became a friend of Abraham Lincoln in Illinois. Commissioned a captain on the Staff of General McClernand's Union Army by President Lincoln, Bielaski died a hero's death at the Battle of Belmont on November 7, 1861.

1834 In March, 234 Lithuanian and Polish insurrectionists were brought to New York aboard an Austrian Man-of-War. American public opinion was very sympathetic to their problems.

St. Joseph's Roman Catholic Parish was founded in Waterbury, Connecticut. It records that the Paplauskas family from Prienai, Suvalkai Province, Lithuania, migrated to Waterbury in 1849.

1838 Among the 1831 rebels to come to America in 1838 were Lieutenant Lucijonas Eismontas, Domininkas Ablamavicius, Barnabas Putramentas, Captain Jeronimas Jagiello, Hipolitas Narusevicius, Kostas Kownacki, Liudvikas Skorupskis, and Rev. Liudvikas Jezykowicz. Rev. Jezykowicz, former professor in Vilnius, was the first Catholic priest to come from Lithuania. He was vicar of St. Andrew's Church in New York (1838-63). Albert Gallatin helped these Polish and Lithuanian emigres to settle down. The United States Congress assigned lands for them in Illinois.

During the Seminole War, on October 20th, the Lithuanian Stefan Augustonovitz (Augustinavicius), trooper of the Second Dragoon Regiment, died of dysentery at Fort Heileman.

1849 During the California Gold Rush, Stanislas Pangauskas, a native of Aluksta, Lithuania, and participant in the

1831 Revolt, after adventures in Australia, came to pan gold in California. He gained a reputation as a rugged prospector. Years later, when he had learned that a new rebellion against the Russian rule had broken out in Lithuania, Pangauskas hurried back to Europe. He was detained by Russian troops on the Polish border in 1864. Sentenced to fifteen years of prison, Pangauskas was able to escape and boarded a ship for Chile. This restless Lithuanian adventurer died on the way.

Due to famine in Lithuania, thirty Samogitians made their way to Hamburg in the hope of taking ship to America. However, due to the intervention of the Prussian authorities, they were detained in Hamburg and then sent back to Lithuania.

1853 The cleric Petras Svotelis came to the United States from Marijampole County, Lithuania.

Aleksander Holinskis, former 1831 rebel and Lithuanian soldier of fortune, after prospecting in the California gold fields, became a United States citizen. He published a book in Brussels, "La California et les Routes Inter-Oceanique."

1854 John Kaczynskis was a successful prospector in the California Gold Rush.

1861-1865 According to the Lithuanian-American historian Constantine Jurgela, 373 Lithuanians (including five officers) fought on the Union side during the Civil War. Lithuanians on the Confederate side numbered forty-two enlisted men and two officers.

Sister Mary Veronica Klimkiewicz, a relative of Kosciuszko, took vows in Baltimore in 1855. During the Civil War she held the distinction of being the first woman army nurse.

1863 Henry Kalussowski, an American citizen and civil servant, was appointed the diplomatic agent of the Insurrectionist government of Poland and Lithuania for securing American aid for the 1863 Rebellion. Kalussowski (Kalusauskas), a member of the 1831 Samogitian rebel movement, had come to the United States in 1838 with his wife and son, Vytautas. In 1850 he started work in the Federal Land Office. At the start of the American Civil War he had planned to form a Polish-Lithuanian legion for the Union. His son, Vytautas, died a soldier for the Union cause. His insurrectionist mission, based in New York, was unsuccessful because Secretary of State Seward favored good relations with Tsarist Russia.

1864 Several Polish deserters from the Russian Navy, including the Lithuanian Miliauskas, who wanted to fight against slavery, were extradited to Russia. This action evoked protests, including a Polish-Lithuanian-Czech demonstration in New York City on September 8, 1864.

1865-1866 After the unsuccessful 1863 Revolt a number of former Lithuanian rebels - priests and nobles fled to America. Among the first to flee Tsarist oppression were Juozas Botyrius, Jonas Staniulis, Vincas Gustaitis and Petras Chmeliauskas. The rebel clergymen included Rev. J. Juskevicius, P. Koncius and Vladas Dembskis. The most famous was Rev. Andrius Strupinskas, a rebel army chaplain. In 1866 he came to America, settling down in a monastery in West Chester, New York. Later, when Lithuanians began settling down in the Pennsylvania anthracite region, he served the religious needs of the Lithuanians of Mount Carmel, Shamokin and Shenandoah. In 1872 he became the pastor of the Lithuanians and Poles of Shenandoah, Pennsylvania.

1867 The Year 1867 can be termed the beginning of the massive waves of Lithuanian immigrants to these shores. The first wave came in 1867-1868 after a severe famine. Another wave of Lithuanians came to America after 1874 when Russia introduced universal military conscription. Many Lithuanian peasants flocked to the United States when grain prices fell after 1885. The Great Russian Famine of 1891-92 drove many Lithuanians to seek jobs in America. The 1904-05 Russo-Japanese War and the 1905 Revolution brought many war protesters and political activists to these shores. The 1906-07 Tsarist reaction in the Russian Empire gave impetus to a new wave of emigration. Prior to 1899 an average of 3000 Lithuanian migrants per annum flocked to America. They came on German, English, and American ships sailing from Hamburg, Bremen, and Libau.

1867 Seven Lithuanians sailed from Hamburg and after three months landed in New York. They went from New York to work on the railroads. Juozas Cernikas and Silvestras Ragaisis went on foot from New York City to the Pennsylvania anthracite region to join Andrius Tepliusis in the mines. Most of the early immigrants were Sudovians and Dzukians from Marijampole, Vilkaviskis, Liudvinavas, Vistytis, Simnas and Liubavas. Most departed from Hamburg. Almost all men came to Pennsylvania to work on the Philadelphia-Reading,

Delaware and Western Lackawanna Railroad lines. Others descended into the mines to dig coal. Still others went to work on the New York farms. The Sudovians were followed by Lithuanians from Samogitia, Dzukija and even Eastern Lithuania.

1869 The first Lithuanian community was established in Danville, Pennsylvania. Upon the bequest of a Lithuanian Jew five Sudovians arrived in Danville to work as tracklayers for the railroad. Jonas Bobinas, Jurgis Reklys, Jozas Slavickas, Raulas and Jurgis Dziaulas arrived in the spring of 1869. By 1872 Danville had 200 Lithuanian settlers.

1870 Lithuanians first settled down in the following cities: Waterbury, Connecticut, Cleveland, and Chicago (Bridgeport and Town of Lake).

1871 The first Lithuanians settled down in Shamokin, Pennsylvania. They formed the Saint Adelbert Mutual Society together with the local Poles.

The first Lithuanians settled in Pittsburgh, Pennsylvania. However, the community started to grow only after 1884.

The nucleus of the Lithuanian community of New York clustered on Mulberry Street. The first meetings were held in J. Budisauskas' saloon. In 1875 the first organization, the St. Casimir Society was set up. After 1880 the colony started to grow.

1872 The Lithuanian community in Detroit was established. The community started to grow after 1880.

1874 Mykolas Tvarauskas of Suvalkai, a former 1864 rebel, published the first Lithuanian language newspaper in America, Lietuwiszka Gazieta in Shamokin, Pennsylvania. He also printed the first Lithuanian language book, an English-Lithuanian dictionary.

1874 The first Lithuanian Roman Catholic Church in America was St. Casimir's of Shenandoah, Pennsylvania. Its first pastor was Rev. A. Strupinskas. However, it was soon taken over by Polish Catholics.

1875 The Lithuanians, together with the Poles, set up the St. Casimir Mutual Benefit Society of New York.

1876 The former Lithuanian estate-owner Julien de Horain (Julijonas Horainis) invited the Polish writer Henryk Sienkiewicz and the actress Elena Modrzreska to visit him in San Francisco. Accepting Horain's invitation the writer Sienkiewicz sojourned in San Francisco; it was here that he received inspiration to use the character of some of the Poles and Lithuanians that he met in his historic novel With Fire And Sword. (See E. Modrzeska, Memories and Impressions, New York, 1910).

1877 The Lithuanian Franciscan friar, Brother Augustine Zeytz (Zaicas) Organized the first purely Lithuanian society, St. George's Society, in Shenandoah, Pennsylvania.

1880 The first settling of Lithuanians in Boston took place. The first organization, St. Casimir's Society, was established in 1889.

Fra. Augustine Zeytz began publication of Lithuanian books in America: Historyia septiniu mokitoiu (Chicago, 1880).

1881 Lithuanians first settled in Baltimore, Maryland. They came from New York. In 1885 the Baltimore Lithuanians established the St. John The Baptist Society.

1883 Mykolas Tvarauskas published two Lithuanian books in New York: Praractwas Michaldos Karalienes is Sabbos and Istorije Ali Babos ir kiaturesdiaszimczio razbainiku.

1884 It was estimated that there were 15,000 Lithuanians in the United States. The first United States Census to designate the Lithuanians as a separate nationality was taken in 1899.

The Chicago Lithuanians established their first organization, the St. George's Benefit Society.

1884-1885 Mykolas Tvardauskas and Jonas Sliupas published a new newspaper, Unija in New York City.

1885 The first truly Lithuanian Roman Catholic church in America was St. Casimir's which was established in Pittston, Pennsylvania.

Jonas Sliupas began publication of his liberal patriotic newspaper, Lietuwiszkas Balsas, in Brooklyn. Later he moved the paper to Shenandoah, Pennsylvania. The paper continued publication until 1889.

A number of Lithuanian organizations were created in major cities: St. Casimir's Society in Pittston, Pennsylvania; St. Casimir's and St. Adelbert's Society in Plymouth, Pennsylvania; St. Casimir's Society in

Waterbury, Connecticut; and St. George's Beneficial Society in Cleveland.

The Worcester, Massachusetts Lithuanians established their first organization, the St. Joseph's Society.

1886 On February 10, Juozas Paukstis and Antanas Pajaujis began publication of the weekly newspaper Wienibe Lietuwniku in Plymouth, Pennsylvania. This newspaper, under the name Vienybe has the distinction of being the longest-lived Lithuanian newspaper in the world.

1886 On April 17, during the meeting of the sponsors of the newspaper, Lietuwiszkas Balsas in Brooklyn, Jonas Sliupas, Pijus Paseckas, P. Ramanauskas, Bucinskas, V. Dziankauskas, and A. Juskevicius conceived of the idea of forming a broad-based society which would encompass all local Lithuanian societies in the United States. Plans were made for calling a conference of local Lithuanian societies in Pennsylvania.

In May writing in Wienibe Lietuwniku Rev. Antanas Varnagiris raised the idea of organizing a Lithuanian Roman Catholic union. Plans were made for calling a conference of local societies.

St. Joseph's Parish was organized in Mahanoy City, Pennsylvania.

On August 15, local Lithuanian societies met and set up the Alliance of All Lithuanians in America (Susivienyjimas Lietuvininku Amerikoje) in Shenandoah, Pennsylvania. Pijus Paseckas was elected the first president. Between 1886 and 1972, this organization, which came to be known as the Lithuanian Alliance of America (SLA) was to have paid $10,000,000 in death benefits and sick benefits to over 100,000 Lithuanian Americans. Its Philantrophic Fund (Tautisku centu fondas) was to pay in worthy charitable and cultural endeavors over $250,000.

On November 22, Lithuanian Catholic societies met in Plymouth, Pennsylvania and formed the Alliance of All Catholic Lithuanian Societies in America (Susivienymas Katalikisku Lietuvisku Draugysciu Amerike). Rev. A Varnagiris was elected the first president, and Juozas Paukstis the first secretary. This fraternal benefit organization became the Lithuanian Roman Catholic Alliance and during its first fifty years paid over four million dollars in death claims and sick benefits.

1887 Lithuanian Roman Catholic parishes were formed in Hazleton and Freeland, Pennsylvania.

The first Lithuanian American band was formed in Shenandoah, Pennsylvania.

1888 There were twelve Lithuanian priests in as many Lithuanian parishes to handle the spiritual needs of immigrants in Pennsylvania.

On July 11, Domininkas T. Backauskas began publication of Saule, an archaic newspaper dedicated to the Polish-Lithuanian Union of yore. Between 1890 and 1905 Backauskas published eighty-five books and brochures in the Lithuanian language. The newspaper Saule ceased publication in 1959.

During the October 30-31 Convention in Mahamoy City, Pennsylvania, the Lithuanian Alliance changed its name to Lietuviskas Susivienymas Amerike. By then Sliupas' Liberals and the Catholics had coalesced into a single fraternal benefit society.

1889 Jonas Sliupas formed the Lithuanian Scientific Society (Mokslo Draugyste) in Baltimore. It published the liberal journal Apszvieta.

Lithuanians began to settle down permanently in Philadelphia. The following year they set up the St. Anthony Society.

In June, Rev. Aleksandras Burba arrived in Shenandoah, Pennsylvania to work among Lithuanian immigrants. That same year he formed a Lithuanian parish. Between 1889 and 1893 Rev. Burba was successful in organizing the Lithuanian Roman Catholics of Pennsylvania into a nationally-conscious community.

The medical doctor Jonas Sliupas and Rev. Aleksandras Burba were the ideological leaders of the late nineteenth century Lithuanian national movement in America. At first the two men worked closely together; however, conflicting ideologies and strong tempers led to the parting of the ways. Dr. Sliupas, an arden freethinker, is credited with founding the laicistic Liberal, Socialist and Nationalist movements among the Lithuanian Americans. Yet this hardworking dynamic journalist, lecturer and organizer did not stay content to work within any narrow group or party. The energetic Reverend Burba served as an ideal for patriotic, social-minded Roman Catholic priests who chose to educate and guide immigrant Catholics from the homeland. Burba was the ideological spokesman for Lithuanian Catholic activists.

On November 4, the Lithuanian Alliance was incorporated in Luzerne County, Pennsylvania, as Susywienymas Lietuvninku Amerike. Vienybe became the official organ of the official organ of the Alliance.

On December 31, the first play in the Lithuanian language by A. Turskis, Be Sumnenes was performed.

1890 "Buffalo Bill" Cody attempted without success to persuade a number of Lithuanians to colonize his land in Wyoming.

There were thirty Lithuanian cultural societies in the United States.

On August 31, the Lithuanian Scientific Society (Lietuviu Mokslo Draugija) formed the first theater group.

1892 Jonas Grinius organized the Lithuanian Theatrical Society in Chicago. Its best performance was "Battle of Grunwald" which ran for four years in the Lithuanian communities.

S. Rokoszas started the weekly Lietuva in Chicago. Antanas Olszewskis purchased the paper the following year. He invited Juozas Adomaitis-Sernas to edit it. It became the leading Lithuanian language newspaper in America. In 1917, J. Bachunas purchased Lietuva. In 1920 the paper closed down in bankruptcy. A. Olszewskis also published 130 Lithuanian books (forty-five originals and eighty-five translations) dealing with popular science and education. These books included A. Lalis' monumental Lithuanian-English and English-Lithuanian Dictionary, J. Sernas' books on ethnography, geography, paleontology, prehistory, and physical science, and four volumes of Dr. Jonas Basanavicius' Lithuanian folklore.

1893 On November 22, the Russian governor of Kaunas ordered a squadron of Cossacks to disperse a crowd of peasants who had gathered to protect the Benedictine Church at Kraziai, Lithuania, from a forced closing. A short and hideous carnage took place. The Cossacks were permitted to rape and pillage Kraziai after the crowd was brutally scattered. After the Kraziai Massacre, Lithuanian-Americans organized mass protest meetings throughout America. They informed the American press about the oppression of the tsarist Russian regime in Lithuania.

1894 L. Ereminas formed the Lietuvos Mildos Giedoriu Draugyste (The Milda Songsters Society of Lithuania), a choral group.

There were fifteen Lithuanian churches, five newspapers and 200 societies in the United States.

Reverend M. Kriauciunas established the first Lithuanian Roman Catholic parochial school in St. George's parish, Chicago. A second parochial school was organized in Pittsburgh, Pennsylvania.

Thirty Lithuanian farmers settled in a colony called Lietuva (Lithuania) near Hazel, Arkansas.

The Reverends A. Kaupas, A. Miliukas and J. Zilinskas formed the Laurynas Ivinskis European-American-Lithuanian Society for the purpose of setting up a Lithuanian-American exhibition at the 1900 World's Fair in Paris. In 1900 this Lithuanian exhibition with its fine collection of Lithuanian books, maps and prints won several gold medals at the Paris Fair.

1896 The Patriotic Lovers of the Fatherland (Tevynes Myletoju Draugija) was established for the purpose of printing books in Lithuanian and shipping them to their brethren in the homeland. By 1900 it had twenty-six chapters and 859 members. During thirty-five years of active publication, it printed forty Lithuanian language books.

Joanna Baltrusaitis completed her medical studies at the Women's Medical College in Baltimore. She was the first Lithuanian-American woman doctor. She was also the first Lithuanian women's organizer.

On January 1, Tevyne appeared in Plymouth as a monthly magazine and organ of the Lithuanian Alliance. Its first editor was Reverend Juozas Zilinskas. In 1900 Tevyne became a weekly newspaper.

1897 Spontaneous demonstrations and strikes were staged by immigrants seeking economic justice in the anthracite fields of Pennsylvania encouraged by the United Mine Workers to attempt to organize the new immigrants. At Lattimore, Pennsylvania, during a strike of Lithuanian, Polish, Slovak and Ukrainian coalminers, the police and mine detectives brutally shot down sixty strikers. Among the dead were five Lithuanians.

The first Lithuanian Evangelical Lutheran Church of Lithuanians was established by Pastor Martynas Keturakaitis in Philadelphia. He also established the first Lithuanian protestant society, the Ziono Dukteru Draugija (The Society of The Daughters Of Zion).

The first Lithuanian American savings and loan association was the Keistutis Loan and Building Association of Chicago. It was incorporated in Illinois in 1901. In 1938 it was taken over by the Federal Savings & Loan Association. In 1949 it changed its name to District Savings and Loan Association. In 1967 it joined the Federal system, changing its name to Union Federal Savings & Loan Association of Chicago with thirty million dollars in assets.

1899 The annual convention of the Lithuanian Alliance of America passed a double protest resolution against Russian political oppression in Lithuania and against President McKinley's military operations against the Philippino nationalists.

Between 1899 and 1926 ten Lithuanian savings and loan associations were created in Chicago as well as one each in Cleveland, Ohio; Kearny, New Jersey; and Philadelphia, Pennsylvania. Their assets totalled over $75,000,000.

1900 Between 1885 and 1900 the Lithuanian-Americans published 198 books in their tongue: fifty-nine were stories, twenty-two histories, fourteen of a religious nature, fourteen almanacs, twelve political treatises, eleven scientific works, eleven dramas, seven handbooks or manuals, six occult or fantasy, three educational and twenty-four general subjects. A book on the question of Lithuanian independence and freedom was published in English, Polish, and Russian. The average number of copies per circulation was 2000, but there were even editions of 3000-4000 or more copies.

On June 3, Dr. Jonas Sliupas organized the Alliance of Lithuanian Freethinkers in Brooklyn, which published books and journals to May of 1915.

During the Boxer Rebellion, A. Sujeta, M. Vosylius, and other Lithuanians served with the American Army in China. These Lithuanian-American soldiers met in China several Lithuanian officers and men serving in the Russian Army. They provided the latter with Lithuanian-American newspapers and books. The publications reached Lithuania unmolested by way of China and the Russian military postal service.

The Society of the Mother (Motinele) was organized by Lithuanian Roman Catholic priests at Scranton, Pennsylvania. The purpose was to provide scholarships to talented and needy Lithuanian Catholic students.

Motinele granted scholarships for nearly fifity years and educated many prominent Catholic scholars and civic leaders. The society published a magazine Motinele.

1901 The sixteenth convention of the Lithuanian Alliance of America, which met in Wilkes Barre, Pennsylvania, on May 21, led to a momentous ideological rift among the Lithuanian-Americans. The liberal national faction came to the convention with many grievances against the predominantly clerical executive board. The first session became heated over mandates and conventional procedures. The meeting split into two opposing factions. The liberal national faction retained the corporate name, charter, and seal. It elected M. Totorius president and chose Vienybe as its official organ.

The Catholic faction met separately and changed its name to Susivienijimas Lietuviu Rymo Kataliku Amerikoje (Lithuanian Roman Catholic Alliance of America), electing A. Tepliusis as its national president. The Roman Catholic Alliance began activities with 784 members. In 1907 it had 4000 members, in 1915, 10,000 members and in 1931, 20,000 members in 304 lodges with assets of 1,200,000 dollars. Its first headquarters were in Wilkes Barre, Pennsylvania. During its first four years it used the Philadelphia Zvaigzde and Chicago Draugas as official organ. In 1917 the Roman Catholic Alliance published its own paper Garsas in Brooklyn. Later the newspaper was moved to Wilkes Barre, Pennsylvania.

Reverend Antanas Varnagiris began publication of the Catholic periodical Zvaigzde in Brooklyn. It was taken over by Reverend Antanas Milukas and moved to Shenandoah, Pennsylvania, and still later to Philadelphia. Zvaigzde ceased publication in 1916, yet Reverend Milukas continued to publish books and reprints of serials which had appeared in the paper. An erudite historian and social thinker Reverend Milukas published 180 books, many of them sourcebooks on Lithuanian American history and social customs.

A Fund calling itself Ausra was set up in Chicago to aid liberal students. This fund functioned until 1910.

1902 Encouraged by Pastor Simanas Pautienius, the Mahanoy City, Pennsylvania Lithuanians raised 100,000 dollars capital and opened the Merchant Banking Trust Company, whose directors were Lithuanians. The bank collapsed in 1933.

1902 Leonas Seporaitis organized a soda bottling company in Pittsburgh, Pennsylvania which made a popular brand of birch beer until 1968.

The first Lithuanian National Catholic Church was formed in Waterbury, Connecticut by Reverend Vincas Delionis (Petraitis). In 1903 similar churches were established in Baltimore and Du Bois, Pennsylvania. By 1913 Lithuanian National Churches were also holding services in Chicago, Pittsburgh, Pennsylvania; Providence, Rhode Island; and Worcester, Massachusetts.

1903 On January 18, through the initiative of Reverend Jakstis, the Lietuviu Ukesu Kliubas was formed in Worcester, Massachusetts. Later it changed its name to The Lithuanian Naturalized Citizens Club.

Anupras Simonavicius set up the Lithuanian Gymnastics Club in Brooklyn. This first Lithuanian-American sports club later changed its name to the Lithuanian Athletic Club.

1905 J. O. Sirvydas began publication of the radical paper Kova, which served to unite Lithuanian socialists. On May 21, a convention was called in Newark, New Jersey. It organized the Lithuanian Socialist Party of America. Dr. Sliupas was one of its founders. In 1907 the party changed its name to the Lithuanian Socialist Union (Lietuviu Socialistu Sajunga).

Between 1905-1918 the Lithuanian Socialists used the Philadelphia based Kova as their official organ. They published several score books and booklets. In 1905 the Socialists set up a printing corporation in South Boston, Massachusetts under Stasys Michelsonas to publish a newspaper Keleivis and Marxist books. In 1908-1909 A. Montvydas published the paper Pirmyn in Minersville, Pennsylvania. In 1911 the Socialist paper Laisve appeared in Brooklyn. A former 1905 revolutionary, Pijus Grigaitis began the publication of Naujienos in 1914. This Chicago newspaper became and still is the second largest daily Lithuanian-language newspaper in America.

Due to Socialist agitation and subversion the National Liberal Society of the Lovers of the Fatherland was disrupted.

1906 Twenty five Lithuanians settled down in Los Angeles, California.

On January 6, the Lithuanian Roman Catholic Alliance of America was given a charter in Luzerne County, Pennsylvania.

On February 22, the first Lithuanian-American political conference took place in Philadelphia. One hundred sixty nine representatives of various organizations participated. The resolutions passed called for constitutional freedom of person, conscience, assembly, and the press to be introduced in Russian and Lithuania, that political autonomy be granted Lithuania with a parliament in Vilnius, that the Russians restore historical and cultural treasures seized from Lithuania, and that political prisoners be granted amnesty.

The first Lithuanian-American protestant newspaper, Tiesos Draugas appeared in Philadelphia.

On the initiative of Reverend Kaupas, the American-Lithuanian Roman Catholic Federation was organized in Pittston, Pennsylvania. It saw its greatest growth during the chairmanship of Reverend Albavicius (1918-1931). This broad-based Catholic federation encompasses all Lithuanian Catholic groups and societies. It engages in educational, social, charitable and cultural activites. The Federation sold bonds during the First World War, held political rallies for the Lithuanian cause, and through the Red Cross provided care packages to Lithuania.

Through the efforts of Bronius Balutis the Lithuanian Society at Valparaiso University, Indiana, was able to institute a Lithuanian language seminar at the University. This was the first instance of Lithuanian being taught as a formal course on the college level in America.

1907 The first Lithuanian-American football player, S. Paukstis was appointed football coach and trainer by the University of Pennsylvania.

The first Lithuanian sisterhood in this country was established in 1907 as the Sisters of the Congregation of St. Casimir in the Diocese of Harrisburg, Pennsylvania at Mt. Carmel. The purpose of the order was to teach religion to Lithuanian children in their own language. At first they were prepared by Mount Saint Mary Seminary in Scranton, Pennsylvania. In 1911 the mother house was transferred to Chicago. In 1915 the Sisters of St. Casimir established a high school which came to be known as the Academy of Green

Tower, Chicago. Eventually the order had 400 sisters, two girls academies, and two large hospitals in Chicago: Holy Cross and Loretto.

In 1907 there were forty-one Lithuanian Roman Catholic parishes with sixty priests. In 1915 there were ninety-five parishes with 116 priests, in 1919 over 100 parishes with 150 clergy. In 1930 there were 150 parishes with 200 priests. One hundred and twenty of these churches were founded and built by the Lithuanians themselves at a cost of 30 million dollars. Professor Kazys Pakstas calculated that it took 200 families or about 1000 individuals to maintain a parish. Therefore, Lithuanian Roman Catholic parishes were not formed in communities of less than 1000 Lithuanians.

1908 J. J. Elijosius-Elias founded the Town-of-Lake Savings Bank in Chicago, which was liquidated in 1920 when it merged with the Universal State Bank of which J. J. Elias was president.

The Lithuanian Alliance of America officially adopted the fraternal lodge system. The Lithuanian Alliance revived Tevyne as its organ. In 1911 the press together with the organization's headquarters was moved to New York City. Tevyne Press published books and four annual almanacs.

On May 25, in Scranton, Pennsylvania, the Tevynes Myletoju Draugija was revived as the Society of Lithuanian Patriots. The first year it formed fifty chapters with 1059 members. By 1917 the society had 4000 members in 128 chapters. The society published the Lithuanian patriot Vincas Kudirka's writings in six volumes. Furthermore, between 1918 and 1925 it printed twelve Lithuanian books.

1909 The Lithuanian born engraver Victor D. Brenner (Baranauskas) designed the United States Lincoln copper penny. Twenty-two million pennies were minted with his initials, V.D.B. before the signature was discovered and removed.

The Boston Lithuanian tailors organized and were chartered as the United Garment Workers of America, Lithuanian Local 149, with 700 members the first year.

Led by Reverend Antanas Staniukynas, the Lithuanian American clergy formed the American Lithuanian Roman Catholic Priests Union.

It concerned itself with forming parish schools and Catholicism among Lithuanian immigrants. During the chairmanship of Reverend Zilinskas in 1920 this organization changed its name to Lithuanian Roman Catholic Priests League of America. It also sought to obtain a Lithuanian bishop for the United States.

On July 12, Reverend Antans Staniukynas began the publication of a weekly Catholic paper Draugas in Wilkes Barre, Pennsylvania. In 1912 the newspaper was moved to Chicago. In 1916 it became the largest Lithuanian-language daily in the Free World. In 1920 the ownership of Draugas passed into the hands of the Lithuanian Marian Fathers.

1910 The first Lithuanian artists exhibit was held in Chicago, displaying for the most part the works of J. Sileika and A. Aleksandravicius. In Philadelphia the Lithuanian Art Association (Lietuviu Dailes Draugija) was formed.

The Lithuanian Alliance of America and other civic organizations lobbied that in the forthcoming United States Census Lithuanians be designated as such and not as Poles, Russians, and Hungarians as before. A Lithuanian delegation from Chicago paid President Taft a visit to petition the matter. Subsequently, President Taft ordered that a Lithuanian category be included in the Census.

1911 The Organists League (Vargonininku Sajunga) was founded in Baltimore. Lithuanian music and composition were advanced by this group of church organists. The League offered mutual assistance to members. The League fostered music and published a monthly journal, Music News (Muzikos Zinios).

1912 The Lithuanian American Medical Association was formed in Chicago. In 1957 it held the first congress of Lithuanian doctors of the United States and Canada.

Alexander Bruce Bialaski, the son of Captain A. Bielaskis of Civil War fame, was the first Director of the Federal Bureau of Investigation (1912-1919). He considered himself a "Lithuanian of Poland."

On August 23-25, Reverend Petras Lapelis formed the American Lithuanian Roman Catholic Student Alliance (Amerikos Lietuviu Rymo Kataliku Moksleiviu Susivienijimas). It was based in Chicago and published the magazine Moksleivis. In 1920 the Alliance changed its name and organ to Giedra.

A laicistic Lithuanian Student Alliance (Lietuviu Moksleiviu Susivienijimas) was organized on September 27-29 in Chicago. Its first chapter was at the University of Valparaiso, Indiana. This Alliance united Lithuanian students who subscribed to liberal, nationalist, and socialist principles. Dr. Jonas Sliupas gave it four columns in his newspaper Laisvoji Mintis. Steponas Biezis edited this section, called Jaunimo Sapnai. In 1915 Jaunoji Lietuva became its organ. The Alliance was active until 1924.

1913 The Lithuanian Marian Fathers organized in Chicago.

Lithuanian garment workers in Brooklyn formed the Lithuanian Tailoring Cooperative which lasted until 1960.

On April 27 and 28, Mykolas A. Norkunas organized the Knights of Lithuania in Lawrence, Massachusetts. A Lithuanian Catholic Action youth organization, the Knights of Lithuania in 1914 had twelve councils with 700 members; in 1915 thirty councils with 1,200 members; and by 1917 it boasted eighty-nine councils with 3,300 members. In 1918 the Knights of Lithuania reached their peak membership: 15,000.

The Temperance League (Blaivininku Sajunga) was founded by the zealous Reverend P. Saurusaitis in Waterbury, Connecticut. Eventually numbering 20,000 members, it was part of the anti-alcoholism movement in the United States. The Lithuanian Temperance League published several pamphlets and conducted many lectures on the danger of alcoholic drink.

The Lithuanian Priest League of America initiated a yearly "Lithuanian Day" at Lakewood Park, Pennsylvania to draw together the numerous Lithuanian Catholics of eastern Pennsylvania. "Lithuanian Day" is still observed at Lakewood Park, Pennsylvania and still draws crowds of 15-20,000 people.

1914 Reverend Fabijonas Kemesis formed the Lithuanian Roman Catholic Charitable Union (Lietuviu Rymu Kataliku Labdaringoji Sajunga). This union founded the five-story Holy Cross Hospital in Marquette Park, Chicago, in 1925.

The Lithuanian Women's Alliance (Moteru Sajunga) was established in Chicago. Its aims were the defense of the Catholic religion and the spread of educational and social activities among Americans of Lithuanian descent. It published weekly the magazine Woman's Field (Moteru Dirva).

Paltanavicius began publication of the national liberal newspaper Amerikos Lietuvis in Worcester, Massachusetts.

Jonas B. Brenza and Jonas Krotkus set up the Metropolitan State Bank with a capital of 25,000 dollars in Chicago. By 1960 the bank had 18,000,000 dollars in assets. In that same year the Brenza family sold its controlling shares of the Metropolitan State Bank.

With the outbreak of World War One, a mass meeting of Lithuanians and Ukrainians was held on August 9th in Philadelphia. It was demanded "that the Muscovites be driven back to Asia and that Lithuania be left to the Lithuanians, and the Ukraine to the Ukrainians."

On September 21 and 22, in conjunction with the fourth Congress of the Lithuanian Roman Catholic Federation, on J. Gabrys' and Reverend F. Kemesis' initiative, a Lithuanian American Political Congress (Seimas) was convened in Chicago, drawing 250 delegates, mostly from Catholic organizations. This Congress called for autonomy on the etnographic principal for Lithuania, the reunion of Lithuania Minor (East Prussia) with Lithuania, and the creation of a national council (Tautos taryba) to coordinate further political activities.

1914 On October 1 and 2, through the initiative of J. O. Sirvydas, nationalist groups led by Dr. J. Sliupas and the Socialist organizations led by Dr. P, Grigaitis met in Brooklyn in a congress, which they designated the Second Lithuanian American National Convention (the first being convened in 1906 in Philadelphia). The Socialists and National Liberals could not agree on concerted programs or action. The Socialists predominated and set up their own Lithuanian Fund (Lietuvos Selpimo Fondas).

On October 3, the moderate Lithuanian groups (liberals and nationalists) met in Brooklyn and formed the American Lithuanian National Party (Amerikos Lietuviu Tautiskoji Partija). Meeting again in Brooklyn, on October 19-22, 1916, this organization changed its name to the Lithuanian National League of America (Amerikos Lietuviu Tautine Sandara). Its middle-of-the road newspapers were Vienybe, Lietuva, and Ateitis. In 1918 the National League established its own organ Sandara (Concord) in South Boston, and later moved it to Chicago.

The Lithuanian National Liberals created the Autonomy Fund (Lietuvos autonomijos fondas). It was later converted to the Lithuanian Independence Fund (Lietuvos Neprigulmybes Fondas) which functioned between 1914 and 1919. In addition, the Lithuanian Roman Catholics founded their own national fund (Tautos Fondas, 1914-1917) with ninety-six chapters, controlled by the American Lithuanian Roman Catholic Federation. The Lithuanian Alliance of America, together with nationalist groups, established a fund to aid Lithuania (Lietuvos Gelbejimo Fondas). The sums raised by these funds were used to aid the Lithuanian Information Bureau in Washington and in Lausanne, Switzerland, to support the Lithuanian Council of America, distribute press releases and memoranda, send a Lithuanian delegation to the Versailles Peace Conference (1919), help war refugees and prisoners of war in Germany, and publish books on Lithuania in Switzerland in French, English, and German.

1915 On February 10, the National Council (Tautos Taryba) was set up in Chicago. Its first chairman was Dr. A. K. Rutkauskas, and its secretary was Reverend F. Kemesis.

On June 10, the Lithuanian Roman Catholic Workmen's League of St. Joseph (Sv. Juozapo Darbininku Sajunga) was founded in Boston. Its purpose was to protect the interests of the working man, to render assistance to him, and to contribute insurance coverage. The League was strong in New England. It published the newspaper Darbininkas (The Worker) in Boston.

Leonas Pruseika organized the Lithuanian Workmen's Literature Society (Lietuviu Darbininku Literaturos Draugija) which published Marxist and progressive works. It was to become the Lithuanian Communist publishing cooperative.

1916 Kazys S. Karpius began the publication of the nationalist newspaper Dirva in Cleveland.

During its convention the Lithuanian Roman Catholic Alliance of America petitioned the Pope to elevate a Lithuanian bishop for the Lithuanian American Catholics.

On September 28, the American Lithuanian National Council set up the Cooperation for the Reconstruction of Lithuania (Lietuvos Atstatymo Bendrove), raising 500,000 dollars in shares for this venture.

Reverend A. Milukas organized the American Relief Fund for Lithuanian War Sufferers. This relief committee consisted of Catholic and Nationalist groups. Cardinal Farley of New York was its honorary chairman. During the summer of 1916 Reverend Milukas conceived of the idea of calling a "Lithuanian Day" in the national capital. A central committee to pursue this project was set up on August 17.

As a result of effective Lithuanian lobbying by Reverend Milukas's central relief committee, President Woodrow Wilson proclaimed November 1, 1916 as Lithuanian Day. Four hundred local committees raised 230,000 dollars for Lithuanian war victims that day.

Between April 1, 1916 and April 1, 1926, the Lithuanian Alliance of America enjoyed a 99.5 percent increase in membership (from 8,920 to 18,321), while assets went from 121,000.00 to 816,000.00 (an increase of 675 percent).

1917 On January 10 to 11, the Lithuanian Council of America called a special conference in Pittsburgh, Pennsylvania Thirty-three Catholic leaders representing the seven major Lithuanian Roman Catholic organizations attended. This conference adopted the first Declaration of Lithuanian Independence (Lietuvos Neprigulmybes Dekleracija) The Pittsburgh Conference delegated Reverend J. Zilius and Dr. J. J. Bielskis to present copies of this declaration to President Wilson and the foreign ambassadors in Washington.

In January various Lithuanian delegations led by Reverend J. Zilius and Dr. J. Bielskis presented President Wilson and foreign ambassadors in Washington with petitions calling for independence for Lithuania.

The Lithuanian Roman Catholic Alliance of America established its headquarters in Brooklyn. This business office was moved to Wilkes Barre, Pennsylvania in 1929.

The Lithuanian Central Committee of America (Amerikos Lietuviu Centralis Komitetas) submitted demands for Lithuanian independence to the United States government and press. These demands were drafted by Judge J. Lopatto and M. Salcius.

In June, the National Council presented a memorandum to the United States government requesting Lithuanian independence.

In June, the Information Bureau of the National Council directed by Dr. J. Bielskis, began operations in Washington, D.C.

When a state of war between the United States and Germany was declared, 30-50,000 Lithuanian Americans answered Uncle Sam's call to arms.

On June 17, Reverend Mickevicius of the Lithuanian National Catholic Church of Lawrence, Massachusetts quarrelled with Bishop Hodur of the Polish National Church. Mickevicius called a popular synod which elected him Lithuanian bishop. He established a seminary for Lithuanian National Church clergymen.

1918 On February 16, meeting in Vilnius, the Lithuanian National Council or Tautos Taryba proclaimed the independence of Lithuania. The news of this act had reverberations in America.

On March 13, the Nationalists and Catholics called the Third National Congress of Lithuanian-Americans in New York. Twelve hundred delegates came to the old Madison Square Garden, New York City, from various organizations. They repeated their approval of the Pittsburgh Declaration of Lithuanian Independence in the "name of 700,000 American Lithuanians" and called for United States recognition of Lithuanian independence. The executive committees of the Nationalist and Roman Catholic councils formed a joint executive committee which on May 3rd visited President Wilson with a petition for recognition. The joint Lithuanian committee also presented a resolution to the President asking him to permit a Lithuanian delegate to attend the Peace Conference.

In demonstration of their loyalty to the United States, Lithuanian-Americans held mass parades on July 4th. Ten thousand Lithuanians paraded in New York City carrying signs to the effect that "Each Lithuanian in spirit is Vytautas and Kosciuszko!"

On October 4, Czech statesman Professor T. Masaryk called a Middle European Union Conference in Washington, D.C. The Lithuanian delegation was headed by Dr. Jonas Sliupas.

Seventeen nationality groups of East-Central Europe attended a political congress in Philadelphia and issued the Captive Nations Declaration calling for national self-determination for the people of East-Central Europe. Dr. Sliupas again headed the Lithuanian delegation.

1919 Lithuanian tailors formed separate locals of the Amalgamated Clothing Workers Union in Baltimore, Boston, Chicago, Philadelphia and New York. They published a magazine Darbas (Work, 1919-1929).

On June 6, a new benefit organization, the American Lithuanian Roman Catholic Women's Alliance, was incorporated in Chicago.

During the National Convention, helf on June 9, in Chicago, the Lithuanian-Americans voted to cast and send to the Republic of Lithuania a Liberty Bell (Laisves Varpas). On August 30, this Bell was sent on a tour of the Lithuanian communities in the United States to raise money and sell Lithuanian bonds. In 1922, this Liberty Bell reached Kaunas, Lithuania, and was installed in the belfrey of the War Museum.

The newly formed Republic of Lithuania was engaged in wars with German freebooters, Russian Bolsheviks, and the Poles who threatened the very existence of the country. The Lithuanian-Americans responded to this threat and began to organize paramilitary organizations such as the Laisves Sargai (Freedom Guards), Amerikos Lietuviu Legionas (Lithuanian American Legion), Amerikos Lietuviu Kareiviu Susivienijimas (Alliance of American Lithuanian Soldiers), composed for the most part of veterans of the American Expeditionary Force to Europe. These would-be volunteers numbered over 5,000, only 500 of them actually went overseas to participate in the Lithuanian Independence wars.

In 1916 to 1917 the radical Social-Democrat Vincas Kapsukas was in the United States agitating support among the Lithuanian Socialists for the Russian Bolsheviks. He succeeded in pursuading a number of Lithuanian Socialists in America to favor Communism. On September 27 to October 1, during the 10th Convention of the Lithuanian American Socialists the left wing voted to close the Socialist Union and form the Lithuanian Communist League of America (Lietuviu Komunistu Sajunga Amerikoje). Led by Antanas Bimba this League joined the Communist Party of America. In 1920 the Communists formed two publishing cooperatives to print their organs Laisve (Freedom, in Brooklyn) and Vilnis (The Wave, in Chicago)

During their national convention in Pittsburgh, the Knights of Lithuania voted to support the paramilitary Lietuvos Laisves Sargai.

1919 On October 1, the United States State Department sent John A. Gate as quasi-diplomatic representative to Kaunas.

The most serious effort to mobilize military volunteers for Lithuania was the establishment on October 19 of the Lithuanian American Brigade by the Military Mission from Lithuania. Colonel Swarthout (who Lithuanianized his name to Juododis) and Colonel Pery were enlisted to organize the brigade.

On December 18 the Lithuanian Freedom Loan Committee was set up to sell Republic of Lithuania Bonds in the United States.

The Joint Executive of the National and Roman Catholic councils decided to petition the president of the United States by raising a million signatures endorsing recognition of the Republic of Lithuania.

1920 On February 18, Jonas Vileisis arrived as the first general quasi-diplomatic representative of the Republic of Lithuania.

On July 3, Jonas Vileisis took the initiative in establishing the Lithuanian Chamber of Commerce in New York City.

The Lithuanian American Stock Company was formed in Kaunas, Lithuania, with capital stock valued at one million lits. Seventy-five percent of the capital investments of Amerikos Lietuviu Akcine Bendrove were contributed by Lithuanian-Americans. The Corporation helped the economic reconstruction of the country by purchasing cars, tractors and trucks for use in Lithuanian agriculture.

1921 On February 16, the Lithuanian American communities first began to observe Lithuanian Independence Day with mass meetings and commemorative gatherings.

On April 15, Vytautas V. Carneckis arrived in the United States as the first official representative of Lithuania.

On May 30, a large delegation representing the Lithuanian Americans presented President Harding with one million signatures in 138 bound volumes asking that the United States recognize the Republic of Lithuania. They also met with Secretary of State Hughes and influential senators and congressmen.

Susanne (Puishis) Shallna received her LL.B. law degree from Boston University. She was the first Lithuanian-American woman lawyer.

On July 13, Clement S. Edwards was appointed American consul to Kaunas, but was not to recognize the Lithuanian Government _de jure_.

On September 8, V. V. Carneckis was recognized as the Charge d'Affaires of Lithuania by Washington.

On November 30, a mass rally representing over one hundred Lithuanian American organizations was held in New York and clamored for United States recognition of the Lithuanian Republic.

The Lithuanian Alliance of America created its scholarship fund in 1921.

1922 The Lithuanian-American Chamber of Commerce was set up in Chicago. Its first chairman was J. Elias-Elijosius, and its first secretary was J. Hertmanavicius.

On July 27 the United States granted _de jure_ recognition to the Republic Of Lithuania. The following day celebration rallies were staged by Lithuanians in Philadelphia and in New York. Charge d'Affaires V. Carneckis was granted full diplomatic courtesies.

According to the statistics of _Naujienos_, the Chicago daily, as a result of the economic crisis of 1922 Lithuanian Americans lost ten million dollars (ninety percent in general investments and ten percent in Lithuanian businesses).

1923 On November 24, Kazys Bizauskas was received in Washington as the new Lithuanian Charge d'Affaires. On June 24, 1924 he was recognized as minister plenipotentiary and envoy extraordinary of the Lithuanian Republic. He stayed at this diplomatic post until August 31, 1927.

Dr. Julius Bielskis was appointed the first consul general of Lithuania with offices in New York.

1924 The Lithuanian Roman Catholic Alliance of America changed its Lithuanian appellation to Lietuviu Romos Kataliku Susivienijimas Amerikoje.

The Sisters of Jesus Crucified were formed in Elmhurst, Pennsylvania. They concerned themselves with caring for the aged and for orphans. In 1945 they moved their mother house to Brockton, Massachusetts, where they also established an academy for girls. The Sisters of Jesus Crucified conducted eight parochial schools. They also have a home for the aged and an orphanage at Elmhurst, Pennsylvania.

On May 20, Mikas Petrauskas' opera Egle, Zalciu Karaliene (Egle, Queen Of Serpents) was performed for the first time in Boston.

At a synod held by the Polish National Catholic Church, J. Gritenas was elected bishop of the Lithuanian National Catholic churches. But the group seceded from the Poles and chose as its head Archbishop Geniotis. These Lithuanian churches accepted the first Four General Councils of the Roman Catholic Church and used the Nicene-Constantinopolitan Creed. The liturgy is in Lithuanian. Supreme authority is vested in a synod. There are parishes in Lawrence, Massachusetts; Scranton, Pittsburgh, Philadelphia, Pennsylvania; and Chicago.

Although cultural exchange groups appeared in the United States from Lithuania as early as 1922, the most popular group was the Dzimdzi-Drimdzi troupe of Viktoras Dineika, Juozas Olsauskas and Antanas Vanagaitis. This troupe literally performed in every Lithuanian community in the United States with song and humor.

1925 The Lithuanian Marian Fathers established Marian Hills College in Hinsdale, Illinois. In 1931 the Marians established Marianapolis College in Thompson, Connecticut for Lithuanian American Catholics.

A Lithuanian group of Sisters of St. Francis obtained permission from the Polish Mother House in 1922 to operate as a separate sisterhood. Aided by Reverend M. Krusas the Lithuanian Sisters of St. Francis opened a mother house at Mount Providence, near Pittsburgh, Pennsylvania. By 1932 there were 150 nuns. Numbering 250, the sisters of St. Francis conduct twenty parochial schools and an academy for girls at Mt. Providence.

1926 The Lithuanian Student Club was organized by Julius and Constantine Jurgela in New York. This club attracted students of Lithuanian descent from New York and New Jersey. The club was liquidated in 1935.

On August 28 the "Lithuanian Day" at the American Sesquicentennial Exposition in Philadelphia drew a crowd of 20,000 who saw Lithuanian folk dancers and choirs perform. A. Pocius conducted the Philadelphia Symphony Orchestra at a Lithuanian music concert during "Lithuanian Day".

1927 As a result of the December 17, 1926 coup d'etat which installed President Antanas Smetona's Nationalist regime in Lithuania, the Lithuanian National League split into two factions during the annual convention. The liberal wing of Sandara supported the ousted President Grinius and condemned the coup d'etat. This wing retained the name National League or Sandara and called its members sandarieciai. The group that endorsed Smetona and his ideological party in Lithuania called themselves "Tautininkai" or Nationalists. They left Sandara and set up a loose organization called the Lithuanian Nationalist Center of America (Amerikos Lietuviu Tautininku Centras). They had the support of four liberal-nationalist newspapers: Dirva, Vienybe, Margutis, and Amerikos Lietuvis. The League retained Sandara.

The offical name of the Lithuanian Alliance of America became its English version. This was officially recorded in a new charter, recorded June 16, 1927 in Luzerne County, Pennsylvania.

1928 Albina Osipavicius, a Lithuanian American from Worcester, Massachusetts, won the one hundred meter swim for the American team during the 1928 Olympic Games in Amsterdam. Miss Osipavicius was to win over sixty-five medals and twelve trophies as a swimmer. She won an Olympic Gold Medal.

Bronius K. Balutis was appointed minister plenipotentiary and envoy extraordinary of Lithuania to Washington. He stayed at this post until May 31, 1934.

1929 According to the Lithuanian geographer and demographer Professor Kazys Pakstas, the Lithuanian American population was estimated to be 650,000 or one-half percent of the United States population in 1929. Professor Pakstas broke down this population by states of which the most populous were: Pennsylvania, 180,000; Illinois, 140,000; New York, 80,000; Massachusetts, 70,000; Connecticut, 40,000; Michigan, 25,000; New Jersey, 20,000; Ohio, 20,000; Wisconsin, 10,000; Indiana, 10,000; and other states, 60,000. The six urban areas with large Lithuanian communities in 1929 were: Chicago, 100,000; New York, 30,000; Philadelphia, Pittsburgh, and Detroit, 15,000 each; and Boston-Cambridge, 12,000.

A treaty of arbitration and consiliation was concluded between the United States and Lithuania.

On the initiative of Juozas Budrikas, the first Lithuanian-language radio program began broadcasts in

Chicago on September 17. This program sponsored by Naujienos newspaper, broadcast every Tuesday evening until 1963.

1930 On February 16, the Lithuanian Legion of America was formed in New York City. The Lithuanian Legion was legally incorporated on December 19, 1935. It was open to all former soldiers and sailors of Lithuanian extraction who had served in the American or Lithuanian armed forces. Constantine Jurgela was the founder and served as Legion Staff Adjutant until 1938. By 1938 the Legion had eight posts in New York, Chicago, Boston, Bridgeport, Waterbury, and New Haven. The first commander was John A. Bucnis, followed by Petras Jurgela and others. After the Second World War, most posts joined the American Legion. The Lithuanian Legion of America was revived in 1951 with posts in Brooklyn, New York; New Britain, Connecticut; and New Haven, Connecticut.

The Lithuanian American communities joined their brethren in the homeland in observing the 500 anniversary of King Vytautas the Great. Observances included song festivals, testimonial dinners, and public meetings.

During the 500th Anniversary of King Vytautas Commemoration in New York, the Lithuanians held their first concert in Carnegie Hall, New York. A music festival conducted by Juozas Zilevicius drew a large audience. This first Lithuanian performance was followed later by concerts performed by the pianist V. Bacevicius, the Ciurlionis Ensemble under the direction of A. Mikulskis, tenor Algirdas Brazis, the Dainava Ensemble, the Baltic States Symphonic Music Concert and other.

A. "Muferis" Zilinskas began the first Lithuanian Radio Program in New York City. He was followed by Vincas Matulevicius, Jonas Dumcius, Jonas Valaitis and, Juozas Ginkus.

The Pirmyn Choir of Chicago under the direction of Kazys Steponavicius-Stephens initiated the performance of famous operas and operettas in Lithuanian translation. Forty operas and operettas were performed by this choir for the Chicago audiences over the years. This choir is still active.

On June 10-11, on the initiative of the Lithuanian general consul in New York Povilas Zadeikis, a conference of local Lithuanian chambers of commerce was convened in New York. This conference formed the National Council of Lithuanian American Chambers of

Commerce (Amerikos Lietuviu Ekonominis Centras), electing as first president Dr. Pranas Puskunigis, and Albinas Treciokas as secretary. Other conferences of this national council followed at intervals: the second conference in 1933 (Chicago), president Justinas Mackevicius; third conference in 1939 (Brooklyn), president Charles K. Pikiel; fourth conference in Chicago (1950), president J. P. Varkala; fifth conference in 1952 (Cleveland), president J. P. Varkala; and sixth conference in 1953 in Chicago, electing A. Rudis president.

The Lithuanian Alliance reached its zenith with 22,332 members organized in ten districts (375 lodges)

The thirty-sixth convention of the Lithuanian Alliance of America took place in Chicago on June 16 to 20th. It was attended by 521 lodge delegates. During this convention the Lithuanian Communists attempted to take over the leadership of the Alliance by machinations and by intimidation (threat of brutal force). The Communists disrupted the first three sessions. During the fourth session the Chicago police were called in to remove the agitators. As a result, the Communist delegates bolted the organization taking with them over 7000 sympathizers and followers in the lodges.

The Lithuanian Communists proceeded to set up their own fraternal benefit society based on the lodge system. On October 14, 1930 the Association of Lithuanian Workers (Lietuviu Darbininku Susivienijimas) was incorporated in New York State. Its first president was Rojus Mizara and its secretary was John Gasiunas. This alliance utilized the newspaper office of Laisve as headquarters in Brooklyn. An official organ Tiesa (The Truth) was issued to members.

1931 From August 11 to 18, the first World Lithuanian Congress was held in Kaunas, Lithuania. Forty delegates came from the United States; they were mostly journalists and clergymen. This congress was called by the Society to Aid Overseas Lithuanians (Draugija uzsienio lietuviams remti) for the purpose of establishing closer ties between the Lithuanian emigrants and the homeland. The chairman of the congress was Rapolas Skipitis, who was also president of the Society. The congress presidium consisted of R. Skipitis, chairman; L. Simutis, vice chairman; M. Krusas, S. Vitaitis, K. Karpius, A. Treciokas and K. Augustas (the latter six were from the United States), A. Vronevskis (from Latvia) and Miss O. Gecionis (from England). This first World Lithuanian Congress drew 105 delegates from thirteen countries as well as Lithuania. The president of the Republic of Lithuania and other prominent personages greeted the congress. Among the cultural, educational and economic decisions made was the resolution to set up a world Lithuanian union (Pasaulio Lietuviu Sajunga). A provisional executive board chairmanned by R. Skipitis was elected. The American members of the board were L. Simutis, S. Vitaitis and Reverend F. Kemesis. A second congress was to be convened in five years. This precursor of the World Lithuanian Community was prevented from growing because of lack of finanical support. The Second World War saw the demise of the union. During 1937-1940, the union published a biweekly journal, Pasaulio Lietuvis, with some financial support from the Lithuanian Government.

1932 On April 11, Antans Vanagaitis began his daily Lithuanian language radio program, Margutis, over Cicero radio. At first this Chicago program lasted fifteen minutes, later thirty minutes, until finally it became a one hour program. Margutis is still broadcast daily in Chicago.

Sophie Barcus began a Lithuanian-language program in Chicago. The Sophie Barcus Hour is still transmitted daily.

Paul and Gertrude Dargis started their Sunday radio hour, the Lithuanian radio program, which still transmits from Pittsburgh and reaches the Lithuanian communities in western Pennsylvania, West Virginia, and eastern Ohio.

Jack Sharkey (Juozas Zukauskas), a Lithuanian American from Binghamton, New York, took the World Boxing Heavyweight championship by defeating Max Schmeling.

Leonas Pruseika (Vabalas) quarrelled with the Lithuanian Communist Central Bureau and bolted the party with his followers. He called a meeting together with Juozas Stilson in Brooklyn. One hundred people attended and helped form the Lietuviu Darbininku Draugija (Lithuanian Workers Society). In three years this revisionist Marxist-Socialist Society had thirty-three lodges and even published a newspaper, Naujoji Gadyne (New Era). Although Pruseika returned to the Communist Party in 1936 and became editor of the Chicago Viltis, the Lietuviu Darbininku Draugija remained an anti-Communist Socialist organization.

The Student League (Studentu Sajunga) was organized at Marianapolis College, Thompson, Connecticut for the purpose of uniting Lithuanian Catholic students in this country for religious and national activities. It published a monthly magazine The Students' Word (Studentu Zodis).

1933 The first permanent Lithuanian folk dance groups were organized by Vytautas Bielajus in Chicago, Lilian Stilson in New York, and Ona Karpius in Cleveland.

As Chicago's World Fair approached, the Lithuanian community planned for a "Lithuanian Day." On June 5, 1933 nine financial, commercial, and industrial Lithuanian leaders met and set up the Lithuanian Professional and Businessmen's Association, which transcended the Chicago Fair and continued the work begun by the Chamber of Commerce. In 1937 this Association expanded to become the Lithuanian Chamber of Commerce of Illinois.

The Chicago Lithuanians set up a world's fair Lithuanian Day committee. A. Mastauskas was chosen chairman, Mrs. S. Bytautas was secretary. The Lithuanian Day program was held on July 16th at the Hall of Science, Chicago World's Fair Grounds. A. S. Pocius conducted a combined chorus of Lithuanian choirs. The ballet troupe of St. Casimir's Academy performed Lithuanian folkdances.

In 1931 two Lithuanian American flyers, Steponas Darius and Stasys Girenas had concived of the idea of flying nonstop to Lithuania. In June, 1932 they had purchased a used Bellanca aeroplane for 3,200 dollars. On July 11, 1932 a meeting had been called at the Lithuanian Consulate in Chicago to set up a popular committee to sponsor the flight. A committee and fund had been set up under the chairman of Consul Antanas Kalvaitis. On July 14, 1932 plans had been drawn up for holding aviation days in the various Lithuanian communities to raise money. The first such Aviation Day had been held on August 7, 1932 in Chicago. A new 388 HP engine had been bought from Wright Aeronautical Company. On January 14, 1933 Darius and Girenas, according to agreement, assigned the aircraft to the Darius-Girenas Fund trustees until they reach Kaunas, Lithuania. The plane was christened Lituanica. On May 7, 1933 Darius and Girenas bid their Chicago supporters farewell and started on the first leg of their flight. They landed in Newark Airport and the following day flew to Floyd Bennet Field. The Lithuanian Americans had raised sufficient funds for the refurbishing of Lituanica and for the necessary fuel and instruments.

On July 15, Stasys Girenas and Steponas Darius took off in Lituanica I in a nonstop flight across the Atlantic from New York to Kaunas, Lithuania. They left Floyd Bennet Field and on July 17, were allegedly shot down by the Nazi Germans near Soldin Forest, Germany. They had flown 3984 miles in thirty-five hours and fifteen minutes. They were 404 miles short of Kaunas. Had they reached Kaunas, they would have broken Wiley Posts flight to Berlin at the same time.

1934 On April 1, Stephen and Valentina Minkus began their radio program in Boston. This program still transmits and is the oldest Lithuanian-language program in New England.

On May 31, 1934 Mikas Bagdonas assumed the post of Charge d'affaires ad interim of Lithuanian in Washington.

On December 14, the Lithuanian Workers Society of St. Joseph began the broadcasts of the "Lithuanian Radio Program" in Boston. This is the second oldest continuous Lithuanian-language program in New England.

1935 According to Lithuanian statistics for 1935, there were over one thousand local mutual benefit societies, providing in most cases only sick and death benefits. There were twenty building and loan associations in Illinois, four in Pennsylvania, three in Maryland, three in New Jersey, one in Ohio, and one in Massachusetts with "predepression" combined assets of about ten million dollars. But there were few large companies and corporations run by Lithuanians in America. The Universal State Bank of Chicago, the Kazemekas Bank of Waterbury, Connecticut, and others disappeared during the Depression. The Metropolitan State Bank of Chicago, the Polithania State Bank of Pittsburgh, and the Savings and Loan Bank of Cleveland successfully weathered the banking difficulties of the Depression and New Deal.

On July 1, Povilas Zadeikis was appointed to the post of minister plenipotentiary and envoy extraordinary of Lithuania to Washington.

On September 21, Felix Vaitkus took off in <u>Lituanica II</u> (a modified Lockheed) from New York for a nonstop to Kaunas. But after twenty-two hours, because of bad weather, he was forced to land in Ireland.

1936 Despite the Depression, the three fraternal benefit societies with their lodges were able to hold their own in the fraternal insurance field. On January 1, the Lithuanian Alliance of America had 13,746 members, the Lithuanian Roman Catholic Alliance of America, 11,720; and the Association of Lithuanian Workers, 5,296.

The Sisters of the Immaculate Conception came to the United States from Lithuania. Their house was established in Putnam, Connecticut. This order conducted retreats for Lithuanian girls.

Pranas (Frank) Lubinas was the captain of the United States Basketball Team during the Berlin Olympic Games of 1936.

The Lithuanian language was taught on a college level at the following schools by Dr. J. Raymond-Rimavicius (Lithuanian language and literature) at Marianapolis College and Columbia University, Professor Carl Darling Buck at the University of Chicago, Professor Samuel H. Cross (Balto-Slavic Philology) at Harvard University, Professor Roland G. Kent (Lithuanian) at the University of Pennsylvania, Professor Harold H. Bender (Lithuanian) at Princeton University, Dr. Edward Prokosch at Yale University (Lithuanian) and Professor Alfred Senn at the University of Pennsylvania.

The jubilee convention of the Lithuanian Alliance of America was held in Cleveland from June 22 to 27. Dr. Jonas Sliupas and other veteran organizers were feted.

1937 Ona Ivaska organized a Lithuanian folk dance group in Boston, which still performs at international festivals and Lithuanian functions.

The following Lithuanian American athletes helped Lithuania train and win the European Basketball Championship in 1937 and 1939: V. Budriunas, Giedraitis, J. Jurgela, J. Knasas, F. Kriauciunas, F. Lubinas, K. Savickas, F. Talzunas, and J. Zukas.

1938 March 15. Poland's ultimatum forced Lithuania to reopen diplomatic relations with Poland. Lithuanian Americans staged mass protest demonstrations in the major cities against the Polish Republic for this threat of force. Resolutions were sent to American statesmen and members of Congress.

1939 On March 21, Hitler forced Lithuania to cede her seaport Klaipeda (Memel) to Germany. Once again the patriotic Lithuanian American organizations held protest meetings and drafted resolutions against Nazi aggression.

Aggression against Lithuania and her neighbors was initiated on August 23, 1939. On that date a nonaggression pact was signed in Moscow between the

Soviet Union and Nazi Germany. Stalin and Hitler conspired against the free world, and on September 1, 1939 the Second World War broke out. A secret protocol was attached to the so-called Ribbentrop-Molotov Pact which outlined the division of Eastern Europe between Germany and Russia. The secret protocol stated in part: " (1) In the event of the territorial and political rearrangement in the areas belonging to the Baltic States (Finland, Estonia, Latvia, Lithuania), the northern boundary of Lithuania shall represent the boundary of the sphere of influence of Germany and the USSR. In this connection the interest of Lithuania in the Vilna area is recognized by each party. (2) In the event of the event of the territorial and political rearrangement of the areas belonging to the Polish State, the spheres of influence of Germany and the USSR shall be bounded approximately by the line of the rivers Narew, Vistula, and San."

On October 10, 1939, the Soviet Union returned the Vilnius region to Lithuania. The Soviet Union demanded the right to station 25,000 troops within Lithuania as a safeguard against aggression.

On October 10, 1939, Lithuania signed a Pact of Mutual Assistance with Russia, largely through restraint and on the threat of dire circumstances if resistance was offered. The Treaty declared in part: Article 7. "The realization of this Treaty must not infringe the sovereign rights of the contracting parties especially the structure of their respective states, their economic and social systems, military instruments and altogether the principle of non-intervention of one State in the internal affairs of another State." In reality, the Soviet garrisons served as a Trojan Horse in Lithuania.

Three or four Lithuanian families settled in Miami, Florida, creating the nucleus of a Lithuanian-American community.

On September 10, "Lithuanian Day" at the New York World's Fair drew tens of thousands to observe thirty-one choirs and 3000 voices perform. The New York newspapers called this nationality day one of the best at the World's Fair.

1940 June 14. Molotov handed the Lithuanian Foreign Minister Urbsys the Soviet ultimatum. Full compliance would mean the end of Lithuanian independence.

June 15. Large Red army formations proceeded to invade Lithuania. President Smetona fled to Germany after having pleaded with his indecisive cabinet for resistance against Soviet aggression. The Soviets occupied the country.

July 15. The United States Treasury Department decided to block all the assets and accounts of the three Baltic states in the United States. The title to the assets remained in the names of the non-Soviet governments of Estonia, Latvia, and Lithuania.

On July 23, 1940, United States Under-Secretary of State Sumner Welles issued a statement condemning the deliberate suppression by "devious process of the independence of the Baltic States.".

On July 30, the American Minister to Kaunas, Owen J. C. Norem, left Lithuania because the United States Government preferred to regard the Sovietization of Lithuania illegal.

The Republic of Lithuania was occupied by the sheer weight of Soviet military might. Guarded by a force of 300,000 Red soldiers, the Kremlin's agents immediately formed a puppet regime and called it the "Lithuanian People's Government." This puppet government, with the help of the Red Army and the Communist Party apparatus, handpicked a so-called "People's Diet" which immediately asked the Kremlin to incorporate Lithuania into the Soviet Union. The Supreme Soviet of the USSR complied on August 3, 1940, and Lithuania was designated a Soviet republic. This was a classical example of outright annexation by an occupying power.

On August 10, the Lithuanian Roman Catholic Federation, convening in Pittsburgh, voted in favor of setting up an inter-group center to fight for the restoration of Lithuania's independence.

In September the Socialists organized a Democratic Lithuanian Independence Alliance.

After preliminary consultations, spokesmen of three major ideological groups - the Socialists, Catholics and Liberal Nationalists (Sandara) formed a delegation to visit Washington and thank President Franklin D. Roosevelt for his condolences to enslaved Lithuania. The president's remarks were optimistic and reassuring.

After the audience, the Lithuanian delegation met at the Lithuanian Legation and decided that the president's favorable remarks had opened the way for further Lithuanian American action concerning the plight of Lithuania. They formed the intergroup Committee to Aid Lithuania (Lietuviai Gelbeti Taryba).

On October 6, Baltic Day was held at the New York World's Fair, at the Court of Peace. The diplomatic representatives of the three occupied Baltic countries spoke at this event. A concert of folk songs of the Estonians, Latvians, and Lithuanians followed.

1941 On March 10, President Antanas Smetona arrived in New York. On April 1, the exiled Lithuanian leader visited Sumner Welles in the State Department. Through the efforts of Minister Zadeikis he had a private audience with President Roosevelt whom he thanked for the United States Government's refusal to recognize Lithuania' occupation.

On May 4, Mayor Edward Kelly of Chicago gave a special reception in honor of the Lithuanian president.

During the May 15th meeting of the Committee to Aid Lithuania in Chicago, it was decided to change the organization's name to Lithuanian American Council (Amerikos Lietuviu Taryba). The executive committee consisted of Chairman Leonardas Simutis, Dr. Pijus Grigaitis, and Mykolas Vaidyla.

President Smetona toured the larger cities where Lithuanians had settled in great numbers: New York, Newark, Elizabeth, Philadelphia, Baltimore, Pittsburgh, Detroit, Cleveland, urging his nationals to organize for liberation.

On June 7 and 8 the Lithuanian Nationalist leaders held a conference in Sodus, Michigan, and decided to form the Lithuanian Liberation Alliance (Lietuvai Vaduoti Sajunga). During 1941, as President Smetona's supporters flocked to the Lithuanian Liberation Alliance, effective action chapters were formed in the Lithuanian communities.

On August 2, Jack J. Stukas began broadcasting his radio program "Memories of Lithuania" to 100,000 listeners in New York, New Jersey and eastern Connecticut. His program still exists.

The first Lithuanian Franciscan, Justinas Vaskys, arrived in Pittsburgh from Europe. In 1944 the exiled Lithuanian Franciscans had a monastery in Greene, Maine. In 1947 they moved to Kennebunkport, Maine, where they set up a monastery, and a high school for boys. In 1949 they established a mission in Bridgeville, Pennsylvania. In 1951 the Lithuanian Franciscans opened up a monastery and press in Brooklyn, New York. They took over the publication of Darbininkas, the former Catholic paper in Boston. They also publish two Catholic magazines Aidai, and Sv. Pranciskaus Varpelis.

During the Second World War, 1941-1945, over 100,000 Lithuanian Americans served in the United States armed forces.

During the summer of 1941 the Lithuanian Cultural Institute was founded in Chicago. Under the leadership of Professor Kazys Pakstas the Institute published books on Lithuania in English, organized lectures and seminars, and established relations with similar institutes of Eastern European background.

1942 J. and A. Andriulis set up the Michigan Farm Cheese Dairy in Fountain, Michigan, and began a successful enterprise processing Lithuanian-style cheeses. By 1958 their company was making 25,000 cheeses a day.

Anthony J. Rudis set up the successful Rockwell Engineering Company in Rockwell, Illinois. Mr. Rudis was the first Lithuanian American industrialist.

1943 On January 8, the Lithuanian American Council held a conference in New York and prepared by-laws, set up a treasury, authorized an executive committee to act in its name. It was incorporated in the State of Illinois. The executive committee was comprised of editors of three ideological newspapers: Leonardas Šimutis (Draugas), Pijus Grigaitis (Naujienos), and Mykolas Vaidyla (Sandara).

On January 8, the Lithuanian American Council issued an appeal to all Lithuanian-Americans to organize local observances of Lithuanian Independence Day on February 16, to solicit prominent American speakers, and to collect contributions for the work of the Council. This appeal has been implemented by Lithuanian communities ever since 1943.

On September 2 and 3, the Lithuanian American Council called a nationwide Lithuanian American Congress in Pittsburgh. It was attended by 400 delegates from various patriotic organizations. Paul P. Dargis was the congress chairman. All of the delegates agreed to put aside their ideological differences and agreed to better relations for the common cause.

The Lithuanian American Council, encouraged by the success of this first Lithuanian American Congress, called seven other congresses to date: in Chicago in 1945; in New York in 1949; in Chicago in 1953; in Boston in 1958; in Washington in 1964; in Detroit in 1969; and in Chicago in 1974.

The Lithuanian American Council on auspicious occasions paid visits to the White House to submit appropriate memoranda to the president, namely: audiences were held with Harry S. Truman (1946, 1948, and 1952), Dwight D. Eisenhower (1953) and John F. Kennedy (1962). Frequent visits were also made to see the then secretaries of state and vice-presidents.

1944 On January 9, President Antanas Smetona of Lithuania died in a fire in the home of his son in Cleveland, Ohio.

On February 5 and 6, during the congress of the Lithuanian Liberation Alliance in New York, a special commission was formed to present the Lithuanian problem to the American public. This commission was designated the Lithuanian American Mission. The executive board consisted of Anthony Olis, Antanas Kumskis and Pius J. Ziurys. This Mission solicited congressment and senators to speak on Lithuania's behalf in Congress during Lithuanian Independence Day and to have their remarks made a public document in the Congressional Record. The Mission also used public relations techniques to obtain coverage in the American press.

In April the Lithuanian American Council set up the Lithuanian American Information Center in New York City to maintain close relations with American senators, congressmen and government officials. The LAIC provided information to the media about the current situation in Lithuania. It published the Lithuanian Bulletin.

Msgr. Francis M. Juras established his cultural archive, which he called ALKA (an acronym which means Amerikos Lietuviu Kulturos Archyvas). In 1951 this rich collection of Lithuanistic materials was deposited with the Sisters of Jesus Crucified in Brockton, Massachusetts. Later the archive was moved to Putnam, where in 1964 the Sisters of the Immaculate Conception housed it in a separate building.

The United Lithuanian Relief Fund of America was organized. The Nationalists (Tautininkai) already had their Lithuanian National Relief Fund which received assistance from the American National War Fund. On March 24, 1944 all Lithuanians joined together - the Catholics, Socialists, Nationalists, and Liberals, and formed the United Lithuanian Relief Fund which was popularly known by its Lithuanian acronym: BALF (Bendrasis Amerikos Lietuviu Salpos Fondas). Msgr. Joseph B. Koncius was elected chairman. BALF became part of the United States President's War Relief Control Board. It joined the National War Fund on July 31, 1944. About 140 local chapters were organized which collected money, clothing and food for war refugees. Between April 1, 1944 and June 30, 1954 BALF received from the Lithuanian Americans 1,470,000.00 dollars in cash, and 2,581,000 lbs. of food, clothing and medicine to distribute to Lithuanian war victims.

Between 1944 and 1947 the Lithuanian Alliance of America and the Lithuanian Roman Catholic Alliance of America converted their life insurance mortality ratios from the National Fraternal Congress Four Percent Tables to the American Experience Three Percent Tables of Mortality. This reform helped establish a more stable mortality experience for these fraternal societies.

On March 21, Vice-President H. S. Truman received the executive board of the Lithuanian American Mission.

On March 23, the Lithuanian American Mission organized a reception in Washington for members of the United States Congress and American statesmen. This banquet reception helped publicize the Lithuanian Question in Washington.

In May, when the United Nations Organization met in San Francisco, the Lithuanian American Mission and the Lithuanian American Council sent delegations of lobbyists who held press conferences and who tried to raise the Lithuanian Question.

BALF sent care packages, medicine and clothing to Lithuanian refugees in Sweden, France, Switzerland, Belgium, Germany, Austria, and Italy, where over 100,000 Lithuanian displaced persons had sought refuge.

There was a threat that the Western Allies would turn Lithuanian refugees over to the Soviets. On August 31, Msgr. Koncius of BALF lodged a formal complaint with the United States War Department that the Soviets were harassing Lithuanian refugees in the western zone of Germany. On November 3, General J. H. Hilding replied and informed BALF that the Lithuanian refugees will not be forcibly repatriated to the East.

On November 29 to December 1, the Lithuanian American Council convened its second congress in Chicago, which was attended by 830 delegates from 250 organizations.

This congress demanded restoration of independence for Lithuania.

1946 The Knights of Lithuania set up a Lithuanian Affairs Committee guided by the dynamic Reverend John C. Jutt-Jutkevicius of Worcester, Massachusetts. Using modern American lobbying and public relations techniques, the Lihtuanian Affairs Committee, over the years, helped mold official and public opinion concerning Lithuania.

In 1946 the World Lithuanian Archive (Pasaulio Lietuviu Archyvas) was started in Germany. In 1951 the Archive was moved to Chicago by its director Vincas Liulevicius. The Cultural Fund of the Lithuanian Community took over the care of the Archive in 1955. In 1964 it was deposited with the Lithuanian Jesuit Youth Center. The World Lithuanian Archive contains over 400,000 units of books, magazines, periodicals, documents, and memorabilia.

On October 26, a delegation of the Lithuanian American Council visited President Truman and asked him to reaffirm the United States policy of non-recognition of the Soviet incorporation of Lithuania. President Truman assured them that United States policy has not changed.

1947 On February 26 to 27 representatives of the Lithuanian American Council and BALF met with Latvian and Estonian representatives in Washington to discuss possibilities of relocating Baltic refugees to the United States.

From November 2 to 6 the BALF convention in New York made a decision to take positive action in bringing the Lithuanian displaced persons to the United States. Reverend Koncius went to Washington on this matter to meet with United States government officials.

1948 On June 28, the United States Congress passed the Displaced Persons Act (Act 774) granting 205,000 displaced persons permission to come to the United States by the end of 1950. Under this law 27,807 Lithuanians came to the United States. BALF had 34,260 guarantees for resettlement.

Public Law No. 774 of the 80th Congress was signed into law by President Harry S. Truman. The essential provisions of this Act enabled the special admission of displaced victims of World War II into the United States without regard to the current quota limitations, but charging them to future quotas of their countries of birth up to fifty percent of the quota per year.

The Lithuanian Jesuit Province was established in Chicago. The Lithuanian Jesuits opened a youth center and published two journals in Lithuanian: Laiskai Lietuviams and Zvaigzde.

Through the efforts of Reverend Kazimieras Matulaitis, the Lithuanian Catholic Press Society was set up in Chicago. A Lithuanian Book Club of subscribers was organized to finance the publication of new works of literature in Lithuanian. By 1970 the Lithuanian Book Club had published seventy literary titles.

On October 30, the USS General Black convoyed 148 Lithuanian displaced persons, the first of 34,000. They were met in New York harbor by representatives of BALF.

Between 1948 and 1953 35-37,000 Lithuanian refugees came to the United States. These newcomers supported the work of old immigrants' organizations and also formed new organizations. They introduced new periodicals and newspapers. Thus, they greatly enriched the cultural activity of Lithuanian-Americans. They organized concerts and folk song and dance festivals. They wrote and published not only works in all genres of literature, but also scientific, philosophical, religious, and educational works in the Lithuanian language.

1949 The first goodwill mission of the Supreme Committee for Liberation of Lithuania (VLIK) to the United States took place between January and May, when Chairman Msgr. Mykolas Krupavicius and the Chairman of the VLIK Executive Council Vaclovas Sidzikauskas visited the United States and Canada. The purpose of the visits was to establish closer contacts with the leading foreign policy officials of the two countries, to discuss problems of Lithuania's liberation with the Lithuanian American Council and visit the larger Lithuanian colonies.

The Lithuanian Evangelical Reform Church Synod was organized in Chicago, representing protestant churches in New York, Waterbury, Boston, Baltimore, and Cleveland.

The Lithuanian Catholic Academic Federation, Ateitis (The Future) was transferred to these shores. The leaders of the ateitininkai sought to establish fraternal relations with the Knights of Lithuania and the Lithuanian Roman Catholic Federation. In a short while the Ateitis Federation established all three traditional branches of organization: high school students, college students and alumni or seniors. Three congresses of the Ateitis Federation were held in Chicago: the Fifth Congress (1954), the Sixth Congress (1960), and the Eight Congress (1970). They publish two periodicals: Ateitis for students, and Gaudeamus for seniors and alumni.

On May 22, the National Lithuanian Society of America (Amerikos Lietuviu Tautine Sajunga) was formed which united the former Nationalistic Lithuanian American Mission, the Nationalist Center, and the Lithuanian Liberation Alliance.

The Lithuanian Opera of Chicago was organized to perform classic operas in Lithuanian translations. In 1953 the Lithuanian Opera of Chicago recorded ten albums with RCA Victor. The first fully staged opera spectacle was "Rigoletto" performed on March 30, 1957. The Opera Company has performed major operas every year since then. In 1969 it performed "Dana," a modern opera about Lithuanian displaced persons camps by J. Gaidelis.

The Committee for Physical Training and Sports (Fizinio Auklejimo ir Sporto Komitetas) or FASK was set up to foster sports and team competition among young Lithuanian-Americans in the various communities. In 1957 FASK joined the Amateur Athletic Union of the United States. In 1958 the organization expanded to include Lithuanian teams and athletes in Canada, assuming the name Lithuanian Athletic Union of North America.

The Representative Committee of Lithuanian Women (Lietuviu Moteru Atstovybe) was established in New York. In 1963 it became the Federation of Lithuanian Women's Clubs, representing clubs in various cities. It became a member of the General Federation of Women's Clubs, the Council of European Women in Exile, and the Baltic Women's Council.

The Lithuanian Scouting Movement was brought over to America. In 1949 the Lithuanian Boy Scouts, Girl Scouts, Girl Seniors and Explorer Scouts, as well as the Academic Scout organization were revived on troop, district and regional bases. The scouting magazine Skautu Aidas was brought over from Europe and continued.

After the Nationalists had rejoined the Lithuanian American Council in November 1948, structural reforms and ratio of representation had to be changed. In 1949 the Lithuanian American Council was reformed. The expanded executive board was to be elected annually. The permanent member-organizations of the Lithuanian American Council were to be the Lithuanian Roman Catholic Federation, the Lithuanian Social Democratic Federation, National Lithuanian Society of America, the National Lithuanian League of America, the Lithuanian Alliance of America, and the Lithuanian Roman Catholic Alliance of America.

1950 During the Fourth Conference of the National Council of Lithuanian Chambers of Commerce in Chicago the name of the organization was changed to American Lithuanian Economic Center.

United States Public Law 555 extended the period for entry of displaced persons into the United States until December 31, 1951. This law permitted the Lithuanians of Klaipeda-Memel to utilize displaced persons' rights.

The Lithuanian Writers Association (Lietuviu Rasytoju Draugija) was brought to the United States. This organization of poets and writers fosters Lithuanian letters. If offers a 1,000 dollar prize for the best Lithuanian literature every year.

The Lithuanian Veterans Association Ramove was established in Chicago. It began publication of a monthly Lithuanian veterans' magazine Karys (The Warrior). This magazine is still published.

On October 8, alumni of the Nationalistic Student corporations and fraternities met in Cleveland and decided to set up a loose organization based on local chapters. This group called itself the Lietuviu Tautinis Akademinis Samburis (the Lithuanian National Academic Assembly).

1951 The Lithuanian American Council was instrumental in the establishment of a Lithuanian Section of the Voice of America. On February 16, 1951 the first Lithuanian broadcast over the VOA took place. The former head of the Lithuanian American Information Center, Dr. Constantine Jurgela, became the director of the Lithuanian Section.

On February 17, the Lithuanistic Institute was set up in Chicago by the Lithuanian Professors Society. This Institute was dedicated to the advancement of studies in the Lithuanian language, geography, ethnology, and history. The first president was Dr. Petras Jonikas.

Through the efforts of Vytautas Kavolis and Vytautas Vardys, the Lithuanian Students Association was formed to encompass all Lithuanians studying in American universities and colleges. In 1953 the association was incorporated in Illinois. Between 1952 and 1959 the LSA published a magazine Studentu Gaires. At its peak this Association had fourteen chapters and 2000 members.

On February 24 and 25 the American Lithuanian Engineers and Architects Association (Amerikos Lietuviu Inzinieriu ir Architektu Sajunga or ALIAS) was established in New York. It soon had chapters in the major cities: New York, Philadelphia, Los Angeles, Chicago, Cleveland, etc. ALIAS was incorporated in Massachusetts in 1956. For a while it organized draftsmen courses in Boston, Chicago, Los Angeles and New York. In 1951 ALIAS began the publication of a bimonthly Lithuanian-language journal, Technikos Zodis.

Between 1951 and 1966 the Lithuanian Alliance of America ran a summer resort hours - SLA Manor - in Atlantic City, New Jersey for members and friendly organizations. The Alliance was the only Lithuanian-American organization, functioning nationally, which maintained such a resort.

Terra Publications was set up in Chicago to publish literary works in Lithuanian.

The daily newspaper Draugas instituted a 1,000 dollar prize for the best literary work in Lithuanian. The prize was awarded annually.

In December the Lithuanian-American communities organized observances of the 700th Anniversary of the Baptism of King Mindaugas. Over 7,000 Lithuanians attended the special religious ceremony in St. Patrick Cathedral, New York, presided over by Cardinal Francis Spellman, in honor of the first Lithuanian king.

The Temporary Organizational Committee of the Lithuanian Community was formed under the chairmanship of Msgr. Jonas Balkunas in 1951. On August 18 and 19 this temporary committee drew up temporary by-laws.

On November 18, 1951 the Lithuanian Community of the United States was formally established during a meeting of prominent cultural and civic leaders in New York City. The Lithuanian Community of Lietuviu Bendruomene agreed to work in the ethnic cultural field, leaving politics and charitable works in America to others.

1952 On February 15, the Lithuanian-American Community, Inc. of the USA was incorporation in Connecticut. The by-laws were promulgated on March 6, setting forth as the organization's purpose: 1) to support the United States Constitution, follow the ideals of democracy and actively participate in American life; 2) to contribute to American society by introducing Lithuanian cultural and national traditions and customs; 3) to preserve Lithuanianism; 4) to maintain ties with Lithuanians outside of the United States, and 5) to support the fight for Lithuanian liberation and aid the suffering Lithuanian nation.

Between 1952 and 1955 the Lithuanian American Community, Inc. organized sixty local chapters and eight regional districts.

The Library of the University of Pennsylvania acquired the Jurgis Saulys collection of 3000 titles in the field of Lithuanian studies, plus ninety boxes of his manuscripts and correspondence with prominent Lithuanians. The library used this Saulys collection as the nucleus for the best Lithuanistics library in the country. By 1973 the collection had acquired the following: language & literature - 2,500 titles, social sciences - 3,500, references and bibliography - 200, fine arts - 200, and religion and church history - 300. A total of 6,700 titles or 8000 volumes.

The Catholic Activist organization, Friends of the Lithuanian Front (Lietuviu Fronto Biciuliai) began setting up chapters in the United States. This political action group organized symposia and study weeks in Kennebunkport, Maine, and Dainava, Michigan. In 1953 the LF set up a book fund and started publishing the political magazine I Laisve (Toward Freedom).

The Sisters of St. Casimir built the modern Maria High School in Marquette Park, Chicago, which soon enrolled 1200 students.

After an agreement was reached by the Lithuanian Minister Povilas Zadeikis and the Committee for a Free Europe, the Lithuanian Advisory Group became the Committee for a Free Lithuania, in order to coordinate its work with similar committees of Soviet-enslaved European nations.

1953 The United States Congress passed the 1953 Refugee Relief Act which permitted an additional 3000 Lithuanian displaced persons to come to America.

The Lithuanian Journalists Association was revived.

The Boston publisher Juozas Kapocius set up the Lithuanian Encyclopedia Press which undertook the publication of a multi-volume encyclopedia in Lithuanian. Five editors coordinated 600 contributors. Between 1953 and 1968 the Lietuviu Enciklopedija appeared in thirty-five volumes with an average of 544 double column pages per volume. In 1969 a thirty-sixth volume of addenda was published. This was the first complete Lithuanian encyclopedia covering all subjects and topics.

On July 27, the United States House Of Representatives passed a resolution by virtue of which the House Baltic Committee was created to investigate the seizure and forced incorporation of Lithuanian into the Soviet Union and the treatment of the Baltic peoples during and following the occupation by the Soviets. Congressman Charles J. Kersten was designated chairman. Later this bipartisan committee was expanded into the Select and Bipartisan House Committee on Communist Aggression.

1954 On May 18 and 19 a conference was held in the Baltic Freedom House in New York, attended by representatives of the Lithuanian American Council, the Supreme Committee for Liberation of Lithuania, the Committee for a Free Lithuania, the Independence League (Nepriklausomybes Talka), and the Lithuanian diplomats. This Lithuanian "Summit Conference" discussed the coordination of efforts to regain independence for Lithuania.

The Lithuanian Roman Catholic Academy of Science was revived in Rome. This Academy soon set up chapters in the United States. The Lithuanian Roman Catholic Academy of Science publishes yearbooks, proceedings of conferences and monographs dealing with various scholarly topics.

The Liberal Independent Students merged with Sviesa Federation (est. 1946) to form the Sviesa-Santara Federation. This loose-knit organization fosters liberal principles, existentialistic thought, and avantgarde art and letters. It publishes a nonperiodic journal Metmenys.

On September 20, the ACEN (Assembly of Captive European Nations) was founded in New York to work for the restoration of self-determination and national independence to the nine countries of East-Central Europe. Based in New York it was comprised of member organizations of Albanian, Bulgarian, Czechoslovak, Estonian, Hungarian, Latvian, Lithuanian, Polish and Rumanian Committees. The Lithuanians were represented by the Committee for a Free Lithuania.

Through the initiative of Pastor Ansas Trakis, the American Lithuanian Evangelical Lutheran Council was set up with affiliates in Chicago, Los Angeles, Collinsville, Illinois; Cleveland, Boston, Detroit, and Brooklyn.

On October 28, the Select House Committee on Communist Aggression submitted to the secretary of state its Third Interim Report. The findings, conclusions and recommendations contained in this report are explicit and categorical: "The Soviet Union is guilty of unprovoked aggression against the Baltic States and inhuman treatment of the population of these enslaved countries.

The International Affairs Section of the Lithuanian Student Association was created for political activities. On November 24, this section began the publication of the quarterly, Lituanus, whose purpose was to inform non-Lithuanian scholars about Lithuania and Lithuanians. Lituanus was first printed in New York and later moved to Chicago, where it still continues to appear periodically.

1955 1955 statistics show that three religious orders of nuns teach in fifty-six Lithuanian Roman Catholic parishes: twenty-nine schools have Sisters of St. Casimir, twenty-two Sisters of St. Francis, and five Jesus Crucified. Each order has its own missions which total fifty-three. Four Lithuanian parishes have high schools administered by these nuns: St. Casimir's in Pittsburgh, DuBois, Pennsylvania; Grand Rapids, Michigan; and Hartford, Connecticut.

The Supreme Committee for Liberation of Lithuania, known by its acronym: VLIK (Vyriausias Lietuvos Islaisvinimo Komitetas) moved its headquarters to America. The Supreme Committee for Liberation of Lithuania was created in Lithuania in 1943 as a result of the underground political activities of the various Lithuanian political parties, which felt the need of a supreme political organ to direct and coordinate all efforts for liberation of Lithuania from Nazi rule. When the Supreme Committee came into existence, Lithuana was a German-occupied country. The Supreme Committee, having united all Lithuanian political forces which were working for the liberation of Lithuania was the only body qualified and able to represent the will of the Lithuanian people. With the threat of a second Soviet invasion, the Supreme Committee went into exile in the summer of 1944.

Even in exile the Supreme Committee continued to exercise the mandate from the subjugated Lithuanian people to represent them abroad. During the partisan struggle of Lithuanian patriots against the forces of the Soviet Russian occupant in 1944 to 1952, the Lithuanian people were once more able to constitute a centralized political and military unit directing all the armed resistance in Lithuania. The representatives of that unit forced their way to the West, and on July 9, 1948, at Baden-Baden, Germany, they signed with the representatives of the Supreme Committee an agreement which provided, among other things, for the following:

The fight for liberation of Lithuania is directed:

a) in the country - by the unit created therein and uniting the entire resistance movement;

b) abroad - by the Supreme Committee for Liberation of Lithuania (and its Executive Council which under present conditions is performing the functions of the Lithuanian Government).

The presence of VLIK in New York City made possible the strengthening of ties with the Lithuanian Minister in Washington, and the establishment of permanent contacts with the United States State Department. While based in the United States, the following Lithuanian leaders have been chairman of VLIK: Msgr. M Krupavicius to November 27, 1955; J. Matulionis to June 1, 1957; A. Trimakas to February 27, 1964; J. Audenas to October 3, 1964; K. Bielinis to November 29, 1964; V. Sidzikauskas to December 10, 1966, and K. Valiunas from December 10, 1966.

The first national elections to the Council of the Lithuanian American Community, Inc. (Bendruomene) were held on May 1, 1955. There were ninety-five candidates; twenty-seven persons were elected to the Council, which met on July 1 and 2, in New York. It formed a presidium and an executive board of seven to serve for three years. The first president was Stasys Barzdukas. The Lithuanian American Community, Inc. proceeded to set up a cultural fund, an educational council, and a cultural information bureau. The following civic leaders have served as presidents of the Lithuanian American Community: Stasys Barzdukas, 1955-1961; Jonas Jasaitis, 1961-1967; Bronius Nainys, 1967-1970; Vytautas Volertas, 1970-1973; and Juozas Gaila, 1973- . The following have served as chairmen of the Council of Bendruomene: J. Slepetys, 1955-1961; S. Barzdukas, 1961-1964; V. Volertas, 1964-1967; J. Kapocius, 1967-1969; Dr. Petras Vileisis, 1969-1970; Vytautas Kamantas, 1970-1973, and Algis Rugienius, 1973 -

On July 2 and 3, former members of the nationalist student fraternity and sorority met in Toronto and decided to revive the Lithuanian Student Corporation:

Neo-Lithuania. The Neolithuanus organized chapters in Boston, Chicago, Detroit, Cleveland, Los Angeles, New York, and Philadelphia. In 1958 they held their first summer camp. On December 17, 1961, Antanas Dirzys organized the alumni as the Korp! Neo Lithuania Filisteriu Sajunga.

The Knights of Lithuania set up a Cultural Committee under Jack J. Stukas to foster Lithuanian cultural traditions. The Knights of Lithuania also introduced a gold medal to be presented to a distinguished American who has helped Lithuania's cause. The first recipient of the K. of L. Gold Medal was Congressman Charles J. Kersten. This medal has been presented to distinguished non-Lithuanians at subsequent annual conventions.

On October 22, the Lithuanian American Roman Catholic Federation purchased 226 acres in Manchester, Michigan. On December 30, the land was incorporated as a nonprofit camp, Dainava. Dainava became the site of innumerable camps and weekend gatherings for youth and cultural organizations.

The Lithuanian Independence Alliance (Lietuvos Nepriklausomybes Talka) was set up in New York to coordinate nationalist and liberal resistance groups not belonging to VLIK. This center consisted of the following political groups: Lithuanian Regeneration Movement (LAS), Freedom Fighters Union (LLK), Lithuanian Resistance Alliance of America (ALRS), and the Lithuanian National Movement (LTS). The first chairman was Vincas Rastenis.

1956 On June 15, Lithuanian American students, under the leadership of Valdas Adamkavicius, collected 40,000 signatures and presented them with a petition to Vice President Richard M. Nixon, urging him to use all means at his disposal to hasten the day of independence for Lithuania.

The Supreme Committee for Liberation of Lithuania began the publication of the ELTA Information Service Bulletin in English.

The Ohio Lithuanian Doctors Society voted to grant an annual prize of 1000 dollars for the best work in art, literature or drama by a Lithuanian American.

On June 30, the Lithuanian American Community Inc., together with its Canadian counterpart, held the First Lithuanian Cultural Congress in Chicago.

On July 1, under the auspices of the Lithuanian American Community Inc., the first Lithuanian Song Festival of America was held in Chicago with thirty-five choirs participating. Subsequent song festivals were held in 1961, 1966, and 1968 in Chicago.

1957 In May the Lithuanian Minister to Washington, Povilas Zadeikis, passed away. This created a vacuum in the representation of the legitimate Republic of Lithuania. Shortly thereafter, the United States Department of State recognized his former subordinate, First Secretary of the Legation Juozas Kajeckas as the Lithuanian charge d'affaires ad interim with full diplomatic accreditation.

Headed by Reverend Walter Jaskievicz, S.J., and Dr. Antanas Vasys, the Lithuanistic Summer Courses were instituted in Fordham University, New York for college credits in the Lithuanian language, literature, history and folklore. Scholarships were offered by Neris Import-Export, the Knights of Lithuania, and the Lithuanian American Community, Inc. These courses were offered every summer until August, 1969.

From July 31 to August 1, the Lithuanian American doctors met with Canadian Lithuanian colleagues in Chicago and formed the Lithuanian Medical Doctors Association of America, with Dr. A. Montvydas as first national chairman.

On December 15, the Lithuanian Historical Society (Lietuviu Istorijos Draugija) was established in Chicago. It organized research and lectures. In 1959 it began publishing the non-periodical magazine of history and related disciplines Tautos Praeitis.

1958 The American Lithuanian Child Care Association (ALVUD) was set up in Chicago. It organized radio lectures, books, children's theater, and playgrounds.

The First Congress of the Lithuanian World Community (Pasaulio Lietuviu Bendruomene) was held in New York City from August 28 to 31. Twenty countries sent representatives. A constitution and bylaws were promulgated. The first elective board was comprised of Lithuanians of Toronto, Canada. The first president of this world-wide organization was Jonas Matulionis.

In August, President Dwight D. Eisenhower issued the Captive Nations Proclamation. The Lithuanian American Council immediately took measures to inform the American public that Lithuania is a captive nation. During the same year, when President Eisenhower invited Soviet

Premier N. Khrushchev to visit the United States, promising a return visit to the USSR, the Lithuanian American Council issued an appeal to the Lithuanian community at large urging mass protest meetings.

On September 27, the Pedagogical Lithuanistic Institute was set up in Chicago, offering a three year course for Lithuanian Saturday School teachers.

1959 The Cultural Fund of the Lithuanian American Community, Inc. set up the Lithuanian Folk Dance Institute (Lietuviu Tautiniu Sokiu Institutas) in Chicago. In 1965 it inaugurated folk dance instructors courses.

Valdas Adamkavicius organized a basketball team for the Lithuanian Athletic Union of North America which toured Latin America and played competitive games with local teams. In 1964 the Lithuanian Athletic Union sponsored a second tour of a special basketball team to Australia.

1960 On April 1, the Lithuanian Catholic Religious Aid, Inc. was organized in Brooklyn, and licensed in New York State for charitable work. This organization sent care packages to destitute Lithuanian Roman Catholic clergy and laity behind the Iron Curtain.

The Professor Juozas Zilevicius Library of Lithuanian Musicology was housed in the Jesuit Youth Center of Chicago. Starting his collection of Lithuanian music and musical memorabilia in 1929, Professor Zilevicius collected over 200,000 items for his library.

1961 Reverend Charles Salatka was nominated and elevated to the post of auxiliary bishop of Grand Rapids, Michigan. Reverend Salatka was the first Lithuanian-American to become a bishop in the United States. In 1968 he was appointed bishop of the diocese of Marquette, Michigan.

Through the initiative of Leonard Valiukas of Los Angeles, a Baltic movement was formed in California called the "Americans for Congressional Action to Free the Baltic States." It soon formed chapters throughout the country. The purpose of this movement was to pass a resolution in the United States Congress urging the President to raise the Baltic Question in the United Nations.

During the September 2 to 3 Convention of the Lithuanian American Community Inc. in New York the by-laws of the Lithuanian Foundation (Lietuviu Fondas) were adopted. This fund was to set up a cultural trust of one million dollars, the annual interest thereof to be used for cultural projects. On March 14, 1962 this

Lithuanian foundation was incorporated in Illinois. Between 1962 and December 10, 1974 the Lithuanian foundation accumulated 1,021,000 dollars in capital and donated 294,000 dollars to cultural and educational endeavors.

1962 During the June 2 to 3 Convention of the Third Council of the Lithuanian American Community, Inc. a decision was made to take an active part in the efforts to restore Lithuanian independence. Furthermore, September was designated "Bendruomene Month" to solicit funds through special observances for cultural and educational activities.

The Lithuanian American Community, Inc. established the Cultural Council under the chairmanship of Prof. Jonas Puzinas to coordinate Lithuanian cultural activities and cultivate the arts.

During its July 29 convention the Lithuanian American Council reformed its structure by enrolling active cultural and youth organizations. The executive council was expanded to eleven persons. However, the same leadership remained at the helm.

1963 The Lithuanian doctors of the United States and Canada met in Chicago and formed the Lithuanian World Doctors Association (Pasaulio ir Amerikos Lietuviu Gydytoju Sajunga). It called upon Lithuanian doctors in South America, Australia, New Zealand, England, and Germany to form chapters and join the association.

A theatrical group a la theater of the absurd was formed in Chicago which called itself "Antras Kaimas" (Second Village). Skits, humorous one-acters and sketches were written by K. Almenas, V. Demereckis, R. Stakauskas and R. Vezys, who also played leading roles. This avantgarde troupe successfully toured Lithuanian circles in Chicago, Detroit, Cleveland, Boston, New York, Omaha, and Los Angeles.

On August 30 and September 1, the Second Congress of the World Lithuanian Community was held in Toronto, Canada. This congress voted to transfer the executive board to Cleveland, Ohio. The new president was Juozas Bachunas of Sodus, Michigan. His executive vice president was Stasys Barzdukas of Cleveland, Ohio.

In November the World Lithuanian Community began the publication of its organ Pasaulio Lietuvis (World Lithuanian) under the editorship of Stasys Barzdukas.

1964 After serving as chairman for twenty years, Msgr. J. Koncius retired from the head of the United Lithuanian Relief Fund (BALF). The new chairman was Reverend V. Martinkus.

On August 23, "Lithuanian Day" was held at Singer Bowl at the New York World's Fair. The program was performed by 1000 singers and 500 folk dancers. The Chairman of the Lithuanian Day Committee was Dr. Jack J. Stukas.

Following the proposal of the "June 22nd Commission," the Supreme Committee for Liberation of Lithuania consolidated its forces with other movements during its November 28 to 29 annual session. The VLIK Council was to be comprised of fifteen groups: seven Lithuanian political parties, seven resistance groups and one so-called cultural-social group. The organization was to consist of three organs: the Seimas (Congress), Taryba (Council), and Valdyba (Executive Board) of seven. Vaclovas Sidzikauskas was elected chairman. The National Fund (Tautos Fondas) was also reformed. Its chairman, Msgr. John Balkunas, was re-elected.

1965 Protesting the 25th anniversary of the Soviet occupation of Lithuania, a grass roots movement initiated by the "new generation" was the Baltic Freedom Rally and March to the United Nations. On June 25, 1965 the Committee to Restore Lithuania's Independence was set up in New York. The executive staff consisted of Anthony B. Mazeika (Chairman), Algirdas Budreckis, Anthony Snieckus, Romas Kezys, Juozas Miklovas, and Msgr. John Balkunas. On November 13, 1965 some 11,000 Lithuanians, Latvians, and Estonians thronged into New York's Madison Square Garden. The principal speakers were Senator Karl E. Mundt (R. So. Dakota); Very Reverend Raymond J. Swords, S.J., president of Holly Cross College; Rep. John J. Rooney (D. New York); and Leo Cherne, executive director of the Research Institute of America. The ensuing march to the United Nations consisted of a train one and half miles long (14,500 marchers). Msgr. J. Balkunas led the mass rally at Dag Hammarskjold Plaza before the United Nations Building in a short prayer. The media covered the event, especially the mass rally. In the weeks that followed, special memoranda were presented to the United Nations missions by delegations of the Committee to Restore Lithuania's Independence. The memoranda explained the current situation in the Baltic States and appealed to the United Nations to restore national sovereignty to the three Baltic republics.

1966 On January 22 and 23, a conference was held in Cleveland, attended by representatives of VLIK, the Lithuanian American Council, the Lithuanian diplomats, the Committee for a Free Lithuania, and the Lithuanian World Community. The political issue discussed was the setting up of a general policy regarding collaboration and cultural exchange with Soviet-occupied Lithuania. Collaboration of any sort with the Soviet regime or its agents was condemned.

On February 12 and 13th the Baltic Appeal to the United Nations - BATUN - was set up by the Lithuanian Anti-Colonial League, and the Latvian and Estonian ad hoc committees that had participated in the November 13 Manifestation of 1965. Delegates of BATUN visited all of the United Nations missions, the three Soviet Missions excepted, and presented the November 13 Petition and other memoranda. BATUN became the Baltic lobby to the United Nations missions. Msgr. John Balkunas was the first president, the Latvian Reverend Norbert Trepsa was the first executive chairman.

Sponsored and organized by the Lithuanian World Community, on June 30 to July 3, the First Lithuanian World Youth Congress was held in Chicago. Attended by 203 students from the United States, thirty-seven from Canada and 100 from Argentina, Australia, Brazil, England, Colombia, Austria, New Zealand, Germany, Sweden, Belgium, Venezuela, France, and Italy, the congress conducted a study week at Dainava, Michigan (June 19-25), followed by a week of seminars and sessions in Chicago. The congress presented a petition with 150,000 signatures from the Free World to the United Nations Secretariat asking for freedom for the Baltic States.

The Stanley Balzekas, Jr. Museum of Lithuanian Culture was established in Chicago. The museum contains a Lithuanistic library, numismatic, philatelic, cartographic and amber collections. It also publishes the Museum Review.

In April a permanent Lithuanian-language TV program was inaugurated over Station WCIU (Channel 26) in Chicago. Broadcasting every Friday evening, the program consists of music, singing, dancing, recitals, poetry reading, and discussion panels. Anatolijus Slutas is the director.

The Lithuanian Roman Catholics contributed to Bishop Vincentas Brizgys' plan to establish a Lithuanian chapel in Washington. Our Lady of Siluva Chapel was consecrated in the National Shrine, Washington, D.C.

on September 4. Vytautas Jonynas, Albinas Elskus, and Vytautas Kasuba executed the architectural and decorative work of this Lithuanian chapel.

The Lithuanian Priests League began the publication of the series Krikscionis Gyvenime (The Christian in Life). It was planned to publish three to four books a year. The editor-in-chief is Msgr. Vytautas Balciunas. The Lithuanian Encyclopedia Press was solicited for the printing.

After a concerted campaign of nearly five years, led by the Americans for Congressional Action to Free the Baltic States, on October 22, the United States House Concurrent Resolution was passed by the Senate of the 89th Congress. House Concurrent Resolution 416 urged the President to: 1) direct the attention of world opinion at the United Nations and at other appropriate international forums and by such means as he deemed appropriate to the denial of the rights of self-determination for the peoples of Estonia, Latvia, and Lithuania, and 2) bring the ofrce of world opinion to bear on behalf of the restoration of these rights to the Baltic people.

During the Lithuanian American Council's annual meeting Leonardas Simutis stepped down from the executive chairmanship after twenty-six years of service. His successor was Antanas Rudis (1966-68). The following civic leaders also served as chairmen of the executive board: Eugenijus Bartkus (1968-70) and Dr. Kazys Bobelis (1970- .)

For his poetic endeavors and his dramatic endictment of conflict, "War's Curse" which was published in the United States Congressional Record, the United Poets Laureate International, meeting in Quezon, Phillippines in 1966, bestowed upon Nadas Rastenis the title of "Honorary Lithuanian American Poet Laureate." In 1967 he was nominated for the Nobel Peace Prize.

1967 On October 21 and 22, the World Lithuanian Political Summit Conference was held in Washington, D.C. on the eve of the 50th anniversary of Lithuanian independence. The conference was attended by the spokesmen for VLIK, the Diplomatic Corps, the Committee for a Free Lithuania, the Lithuanian American Council, and the Lithuanian World Community together with the Lithuanian Communities Inc. (Bendruomenes) of the United States and Canada. The editors of the major Lithuanian-language newspapers in the United States and Canada also attended.

1968 The Lithuanian American Community, Inc. had seventy local chapters organized into regional districts designated: Chicago, Ohio, Boston, Hartford, New York, New Jersey, Southern Atlantic, and Western.

There are thirty-eight Lithuanian-language Saturday schools in the United States with 3,100 students. The Lithuanian American Community Inc. coordinates the curriculum and sets up the standard textbooks to be used.

A conference on Baltic linguistics was held at Pennsylvania State University. It was devoted to topics dealing with the Lithuanian, Latvian, and extinct Old Prussian languages.

From July 8 to 20th the Fifth Jamboree of the Lithuanian Scout Association was held in Camp Rakas, Custer, Michigan. It was attended by 1,600 Lithuanian boy and girl scouts and scouters.

The Third Congress of the Lithuanian World Community was held in New York City on August 29 through September 2. This congress featured the first Lithuanian concert in Lincoln Center for the Performing Arts. Juozas Bachunas was re-elected president, and Stasys Barzdukas Executive vice president. When J. Bachunas passed away on January 1, 1969, S. Barzdukas assumed the presidency.

BATUN organized demonstrations at the United Nations in New York City during the Soviet invasion of Czechoslovakia. BATUN also initiated a massive letter-writing and petition-signing campaign directed at the world heads of state on the occasion of the 50th anniversary of the establishment of the Republics of Estonia, Latvia, and Lithuania.

From November 27 to December 1st, the first Lithuanian Theater Festival was held in Chicago under the direction of the Lithuanian American Community Inc. The following theatrical groups participated with plays and sketches: the Chicago Lithuanian Youth Theater, The Cleveland Theater, the Detroit Amateur Drama Assembly, the Chicago Riflemen's Theater, the Aurora Theater of Hamilton, Canada, and the Los Angeles Drama Assembly.

From November 28 to December 1, the Association for the Advancement of Baltic Studies, Inc. was established by the 150 Baltic scholars attending the First Conference on Baltic Studies, held at the University of Maryland, College Park, Maryland. The first president was the Latvian scholar Dr. Gundars J. King. In 1969 the Association began publication of the Journal of Baltic Studies.

1969 There are 1,650,000 Americans of Lithuanian descent in the United States. The vast majority are of third, fourth, and fifth generations.

Juozas Kapocius began the preparation of a six-volume Lithuanistic encyclopedia in English, entitled Encyclopedia Lithuanica. By the middle of 1973 the first three volumes appeared. The chief editor is the historian Professor Simas Suziedelis.

1970 On July 7, Pope Paul IV consecrated the Lithuanian Chapel "Mater Miseracordiae" in St. Peter's Basilica, Vatican. Most of the contributors to this chapel were Lithuanian Americans. A large number of them attended the consecration.

BATUN organized the Baltic Folk Festival on the Latvian site, Priedaine, in Hightstown, New Jersey. This was the first of a series of annual events to provide opportunities for Americans of Baltic descent on the eastern seaboard to strengthen their social and cultural ties.

On October 18, Baltic demonstrations took place at the United Nations in New York City on the occasion of the 25th anniversary of the UNO. The purpose of the demonstrations was to draw attention to the denial of human rights and self-determination in the Baltic nations. The Baltic Youth for Freedom, an ad hock group of young Americans of Estonian, Latvian, and Lithuanian descent, staged the demonstrations. The Baltic Youth for Freedom responded quickly to current events and drew public attention on the occasions of the Soviet invasion of Czechoslovakia, the extradition of Simas Kudirka (see infra.), Lithuanian student riots in Kaunas, Lithuania, the Soviet art exhibit at the New York Metropolitan Museum of Art, and the visit of Leonid Brezhnev to Washington.

On October 25, the Baltic Youth for Freedom protested at the editorial offices of the New York Times because of the continued reticence on the part of New York newspapers to report Baltic events.

On November 9, Vytautas Simokaitis together with his pregnant wife Grazina attempted to escape to freedom by diverting a Soviet plane from Vilnius to Sweden. The Simokaitis scheme was foiled and Vytautas was sentenced to fifteen years in a corrective labor camp, while his wife received three years imprisonment. The Supreme Committee for Liberation of Lithuania, the Lithuanian American Council, the Lithuanian American Community Inc. and BATUN rallied public opinion in support of the Simokaitis family. Visits were made to the State Department and to United Nations missions in an attempt to commute the harsh Soviet sentence.

On November 23, a Lithuanian seaman, Simas Kudirka, defected from the Soviet Trawler Sovietskaya Litva off Martha's Vineyard, Massachusetts. S. Kudirka boarded the adjacent U.S. Coast Guard cutter Vigilant and asked for political asylum. After eight hours, upon the advice of the United States State Department to the Coast Guard Authorities, who in turn instructed the cutter to turn Kudirka over to the Soviets. A civilian eyewitness, the Latvian-American Roberts M. Bieze was instrumental in bringing this incident to the attention of the American press. The Lithuanian-American communities were in an uproar, ad hoc committees were set up which generated mass demonstrations. Two Coast Guard officials, as a result, were retired from service. A more precise directive concerning political asylum in the United States was formulated by Washington. Simas Kudirka was subsequently sentenced to ten years hard labor in the USSR. Sustained action to secure Kudirka's release was sponsored by the Lithuanian American Community Inc. which gave financial assistance to Daiva Kezys' Americans for Simas Committee and to the Seamen's Educational Federation to seek means of helping Kudirka. Their efforts saw fruition when in July, 1974 the United States ruled that Simas Kudirka was a United States citizen by virtue of having an American-born mother. The Soviets released him from prison in August, 1974 and permitted him to return to Lithuania.

1971 On January 16 to 17th, in view of recent developments in Soviet-occupied Lithuania, the Council of the Lithuanian American Community Inc. meeting in Philadelphia decided to become involved in political action. A public affairs council was set up under Vice-Chairman Algimantas S. Gecys. By 1973 the Public Affairs Council had eighteen affiliate chapters or commissions that worked under the aegis of the local chapters of the Lithuanian American Community Inc.

BATUN delivered a petition with thirteen thousand signatures to the United Nations High Commission for Refugees asking for the release of Simas Kudirka.

February 16, due to the efforts of the Lithuanian American Community Inc. and the Lithuanian American Council, over one hundred legislators spoke in the United States Congress on the occasion of the Fifty-third anniversary of Lithuanian Independence.

On March 27, the Lithuanian American Community Inc. together with similar Latvian and Estonian organizations sponsored the first Baltic Information Seminar in New York City.

On April 26, representatives of the Lithuanian American Community Inc., joined with Estonians and Latvians to confer with Radio Liberty directors about the possibility of broadcasting in the native languages to the Baltic States.

The Lithuanian American Community Inc. led action to support Senator Richard S. Schweiker's Ethnic Heritage Bill which would provide Federal funds for ethnic minority projects. The Lithuanian American Community also participated in the Washington conference of the Confederation of American Ethnic Groups. Close relations with the National Center for Ethnic and Urban Affairs were established.

The Lithuanian American Community Inc. organized protests in Washington and Los Angeles against the Soviet Exhibition "Arts and Crafts in Ancient Times and Today" because this propaganda tour depicted the Baltic nations as part of Soviet Russian culture. The Los Angeles Lithuanian Community Chapter received good coverage in the local press and television during its demonstration.

The Lithuanian American Community Inc. organized demonstrations and solicited support for the imprisoned Simokaitis family. Declarations supporting the Simokaitis were obtained from the famed labor leader George Meany, Cardinal Krol of Philadelphia, the Metropolitan Council of Churches of Philadelphia, the Lutheran synod of Pennsylvania, Dr. Benjamin Spock, Bnai Brith, the Polish American Congress, the Republican National Committee, and Dr. L. Dobriansky of the Captive Nations Week Committee.

On November 1, through the initiative of the Lithuanian American Community Inc., shortwave radio broadcasts were transmitted to Soviet fishing vessels off the American shores. Fourteen Atlantic coast radio stations participated transmitting news about the plight of the Lithuanian seaman Simas Kudirka. On December 1, in coordination with the Seaman's Educational Federation, leaflets concerning Simas Kudirka were air-dropped over Soviet fishing vessels.

On December 11 and 12, the Lithuanian American Community Inc. sponsored a political studies weekend seminar in Philadelphia. Fourteen speakers, among them Deputy Director for East European Affairs Doyle V. Martin of the United States State Department, addressed themselves to the status of the Baltic Question in international affairs.

1972 Between December 1971 and January 1972, 17,054 Catholics of the Prienai region in Lithuania signed a petition to Leonard Brezhnev, first secretary of the Communist Party USSR, and to Kurt Waldheim, secretary general of the United Nations, complaining that they were denied religious freedom and suffered various forms of discrimination in their daily lives. This action was followed by intensified repression of Catholic bishops and priests in Lithuania. Demonstrations in Kaunas on May 18 and 19 protested this religious persecution. The Lithuanian American Community Inc. sent a delegation on May 31 to meet with Cardinal John Krol, president of the National Conference of Catholic Bishops, and Bishop John J. Dougherty, chairman of the Committee for International Affairs of the United States Catholic Conference. As a result of this delegation's visit, the cardinal and bishop issued a joint proclamation to the following effect:

"In view of these and other equally disturbing reports and in a spirit of brotherly unity with our fellow Catholics in Lithuania and with the Lithuanian-American Community we must in conscience censure the suppression of human rights and freedom in Lithuania and elsewhere. We encourage our churches in this country to join the Lithuanian-Americans in a Day of Prayer for the Church in Lithuania on June 18, 1972. We alert the churches and agencies of the international community to the grave violations of justice and human rights in Lithuania and encourage their support of corrective measures in that troubled country and wherever such violations occur." Similar declarations were issued by Cardinal Shenan of Baltimore, Bishop McNulty of Buffalo, Archbishop Boland of Newark, Cardinal Cody of Chicago, Bishop Grateman of Sioux City, Bishop Hogan of Rochester, and Bishop Sheenan of Omaha.

On February 16, ninety-two legislators spoke on the occasion of the 54th anniversary of Lithuanian Independence in the United States Congress.

On April 13, through the efforts of the Lithuanian American Community Inc., a reception was held in the

Capitol in Washington for members of Congress. Twenty-six senators and forty representatives attended. Three television channels filmed the reception, and articles appeared in the Washington Post, Baltimore Sun, and other newspapers.

On May 14, a twenty-year old student, Romas Kalanta, set fire to himself in Kaunas crying: "Freedom, freedom, freedom! Freedom for Lithuania!" Kalanta committed self-immolation to draw world attention to Lithuania's plight on the occasion of President Nixon's trip to Moscow. For two days after Kalanta's funeral, on May 18 and 19, several thousand youths, shouting "Freedom for Lithuania" swept through Kaunas. On the second day strikes broke out. A sit-down strike was staged in the new synthetics factory. Eventually paratroopers were called in. One Soviet militiaman and one student were killed, several hundred demonstrators were injured or arrested.

VLIK, the Lithuanian American Council and the Committee for a Free Lithuania contacted the United States Department of State and members of the United States Congress on this incident. BATUN organized visits to the United Nations missions in New York with an appropriate memorandum.

The Lithuanian American Community Inc. declared June 15th a "Day of Mourning" for Romas Kalanta, Associated Press and the Media were given detailed information about the Kalanta self-immolation. Senate Minority Leader Hugh Scott conveyed the memorandum of the Lithuanian American Community Inc. to Secretary of State Rogers and to Dr. Henry Kissinger, chairman of the National Security Council. A reply was received from Dr. Kissinger on July 10. A delegation of the Lithuanian American Community visited the State Department concerning the Kalanta incident and asked that President Nixon, visiting in Moscow, be informed.

Under the sponsorship of the Lithuanian World Community, the Second Lithuanian World Youth Congress was held in the United States between June 24 and July 16. Two-hundred-fifty delegates (half from the United States and Canada) met at the Conrad Hilton in Chicago for meetings and symposia. Afterwards they adjourned to Kent State University, Ohio, for discussion seminars. After that a camp was set up in Romuva with the closing in Toronto, Canada. The Second Lithuanian Youth Congress voted to establish a Lithuanian World Youth Federation (Pasaulio Lietuviu Jaunimo Sajunga), under the aegis of the Lithuanian World Community. Antanas Saulaitis, S.J., was elected first chairman of the executive committee.

On June 26 and 29, the 57th Biennial Convention of the Lithuanian Alliance of America took place in Miami Beach, Florida. This was the first instance in Lithuanian-American history that a nation-wide organization held a major convention in that resort city.

On July 1, the Fourth Lithuanian Folk Dance Festival, sponsored by the Lithuanian American Community Inc., was held in the Chicago Amphitheater. The First Lady, Mrs. Richard M. Nixon, was the guest of honor.

The Sixty-fifth convention of the Lithuanian Roman Catholic Alliance of America was held in Chicago between July 30 and August 2. After holding the presidency for thirty-eight years, Leonardas Simutis stepped down. His successor was Thomas E. Macke, the first American-born Lithuanian to hold the highest office in that organization.

On September 14, a delegation of the Lithuanian American Community Inc. visited the State Department and lodged a protest against the visit of United States Consul Culver Glyesteen to Vilnius and his meeting with so-called officials of Soviet Lithuania. The delegation also contacted members of Congress and Dr. Kissinger. As a result, the United States State Department reiterated! the American principle of non-recognition of the incorporation of the Baltic States into the USSR.

In October a delegation of the Lithuanian American Community Inc. was received by Archbishop Luigi Raimondi, apostolic delegate of the Vatican in Washington. The apostolic delegate was given a memorandum about religious persecution on Lithuanian and asked to intervene with the Holy See for a Day of Prayer for the silent Church in Lithuania.

In order to coordinate Baltic political action, the Supreme Committee for Liberation of Lithuania joined with the Free World Latvian Federation and the World Estonian Council to form the Baltic World Conference in New York on November 18. The chairman of VLIK, Dr. Kestutis Valiunas, was elected the first president.

On December 14, a delegation of the Lithuanian American Community Inc. visited the State Department and pointed discrepancies between avowed United States policy and department actions to E. Hurwitz and the United States Chief Geographer· R. Hodgson. A positive result of this meeting was that henceforth United States Department of State official maps would delineate the Baltic Republics and state that the United

States does not recognize their incorporation into the Soviet Union.

According to the Fraternal Monitor Yearbook for 1973, the status of the three Lithuanian fraternal benefit societies on December 31, 1972 was: Association of Lithuanian Workers, Ozone Park, New York, membership: 3,247 and 100 lodges, insurance in force 1,786,479 dollars; Lithuanian Alliance of America, New York, membership: 7,710 and 270 lodges, insurance in force 9,381,045 dollars; Lithuanian Roman Catholic Alliance of America, Wilkes Barre, Pennsylvania, membership 5,138 and 163 lodges, insurance in force 4,027,611 dollars.

1973 On the occasion of the 55th anniversary of Lithuanian Independence eighty-one legislators spoke in the United States Congress.

On February 15, a delegation of the Lithuanian American Community Inc. met with Michael P. Balzano, special adviser to President Nixon, and presented him with copies of documents recording religious persecution in Soviet-occupied Lithuania for the years 1971 and 1972.

On April 24, Dr. Gerald R. Livingston of the National Security Council received a delegation of the Lithuanian American Community Inc. in the White House. The delegation submitted a memorandum addressed to Dr. H. Kissinger that the international status of the Baltic states not be compromised at the forthcoming European Security Conference by making concessions to the Soviet Union.

From July 1 to 4, during the European Security Conference in Helsinki, Finland, a nine-man delegation of the Baltic World Conference attended for the purpose of distributing memoranda on the Baltic Question to diplomats and journalists. On July 5, at the request of the Soviet Delegation, the Finnish authorities detained the nine Balts. Estonian, Latvian and Lithuanian political groups immediately took action to secure their release. Following Secretary of State Rogers' telephone communique to the Finnish Foreign Ministry the nine Balts were released on July 6.

The Fourth Congress of the Lithuanian World Community was held in Washington, D.C., from August 30 to September 2nd. Bronius Nainys of Chicago was elected president.

On August 31, a delegation of the Lithuanian American Community Inc. spoke with the American Revolution Bicentennial Commission in Washington about participation in the Bicentennial. The Commission registered the Lithuanian American Community Inc. as the participating Lithuanian organization.

On October 6 and 7th the convention of the Seventh Council of the Lithuanian American Community met in Detroit; it elected Juozas Gaila as the new president.

The Second Lithuanian Symposium on Arts and Science was held in Chicago from November 21 to 25th. The sponsoring organizations were the World Lithuanian Association of Engineers and Architects, the Lithuanian American Association of Engineers and Architects, the Lithuanian Studies Institute, the Lithuanian World Doctors Association, and similar professional groups.

A meeting of Lithuanian youth leaders was called by the Lithuanian American Community Inc. in Cleveland and as a result from December 28 to 31st the Lithuanian Youth Association of America was established for the purpose of organizing students and other young people of Lithuanian descent.

1974 On February 11, Vice President Gerald Ford received a delegation of the Lithuanian American Community Inc. in the White House. This was the first reception of a Lithuanian civic group on the anniversary of Lithuanian Independence Day in the White House during the Nixon Administration.

From May 16 to 19th the Fourth Baltic Studies Conference was held in Chicago, attracting an attendance of 360 Baltic scholars. The Association for Advancement of Baltic Studies and the conference was presided over by Professor Rimvydas Silbajoris, a Lithuanian.

On June 5 the Lithuanian American Community Inc., in conjunction with Lithuanian Youth Association of America, organized visits to 171 Congressional offices, conferring with nine Senators and nineteen Representatives. The topics of discussion included the status of the Baltic states during the forthcoming European Security Conference. The Lithuanian delegations sought support for the resolutions of Congressman Derwinski and Senator Curtis which uphold the principle of nonrecognition of the incorporation of the Baltic states into the Soviet Union.

The Eighth Lithuanian American Congress was convened in Chicago from September 27 to 29th to deliberate the continued political action of the Lithuanian American Council.

Following consultations with other political centers on March 23, the Supreme Committee for Liberation of Lithuania held a conference to plan the ultimate liberation of Lithuania. This conference took place on October 26 and 27 in White Plains, New York. It was attended by VLIK, the Lithuanian American Council, Lithuanian diplomats, the Committee for a Free Lithuania, the Lithuanian World Community, the Lithuanian Community Inc. of Canada, and the Lithuanian American Community Inc. The conference rededicated itself to the unequivocal restoration of Lithuanian independence. The conference also reformulated its stand on relations with the occupied homeland.

The Lithuanian American Community Inc. together with the Americans for Simas worked closely with Amnesty International, Congressman Hanrahan, and Senator Percy in obtaining exit visas for Simas Kudirka and his family to come to the United States. On November 5, Simas Kudirka arrived at J. F. Kennedy International Airport, New York, with his wife, two children, and mother. They were greeted by Consul General A. Simutis and representatives of Lithuanian organizations. Temporarily sheltered by Dr. R. Paegle, S. Kudirka toured the major Lithuanian centers in New York, Chicago, Boston, Hartford, Cleveland, Detroit, Toronto, Los Angeles, and others. He was feted by local officials and interviewed by the American media.

From November 27 to December 2, the Third Lithuanian Theater Festival was held in Chicago. The chairman of the Cultural Council of the Lithuanian American Community Inc., Anatolijus Kairys, directed this series of dramatic performances.

The annual convention of the Supreme Committee for Liberation of Lithuania met in Boston, Massachusetts for the first time on December 7 and 8. Simas Kudirka was feted at a banquet which drew hundreds of Massachusetts Lithuanian civic and cultural leaders.

1975 The efforts of the Lithuanian American Community Inc. during 1974 to have a one hundred thousand dollar sum included in the 1975 fiscal budget of Radio Liberty for Lithuanian language broadcasts met with success. On January 5, the first weekly boradcast in Lithuanian was broadcast to Lithuania over the Radio Liberty Station in Munich. A daily program was instituted on March 1. A Lithuanian radio staff under the direction of J. B. Laucka was set up.

DOCUMENTS

## THE FIRST LITHUANIANS IN AMERICA:

## "FIRST SCHOOLMASTER OF NEW YORK"

## 1659-1661

Over three centuries separate the New Amsterdam Lithuanians from the present day community numbering over 100,000 in Manhattan, Brooklyn, and Queens, New York. Little is known about the early soldiers and settlers; yet one of them, Alexander Cursius, emerges as a teacher and physician in the Dutch colony.

Source: (From Anicetas Simutis, in Lituanus, Vol. 5, No. 4)

Three hundred and fifty years ago, Henry Hudson entered New York Bay on the "half Moon" in search of the "Northwest Passage." Fifty years later - in 1659 - when New York was still a small trading post of the Netherlands with fewer than 200 houses and about 1,500 inhabitants, the first school of higher education was opened in New Amsterdam (now New York). Its first schoolmaster was Dr. Alexander Carolus Curtius, a Lithuanian nobleman and former professor in Lithuania. Why should a Lithuanian professor have left his country in order to go to an unknown and remote land to become a schoolmaster? Was he a political refugee, a man seeking freedom and a better future in the new land? Or was he, perhaps, simply an adventurer? A close scrutiny of contemporary history of Europe and New York gives some interesting insights into these possibilities.

In the middle of the seventeenth century the expanding Russian empire under Alexius Mikhailovich (1629-1676) became a grave threat to the weakened Polish-Lithuanian Commonwealth. In 1654 the Russian army entered Lithuania, sacking and plundering every town on its way. An eyewitness wrote on July 24, 1654: "Traveling to Kaluga we saw great multitudes of carts crowded with women and children from Lithuania being moved to the East. Men having been either killed on the spot by Moscovites or drowned in the rivers. Seven, eight boys or girls could be bought for one rouble..."

The approaching Russian army brought in those days great panic to Vilnius and the rest of Lithuania....Fleeing professors of the Jesuit Academy of Vilnius tried to save not only themselves, but the cultural treasures as well. The library of the Academy, one of the richest in Eastern Europe, was moved in 1655 to Koenigsberg, Lithuania Minor (East Prussia), and was not returned to Vilnius until the Russians were driven out. Prussia and Western Europe were flooded with Lithuanian refugees, some going as far as Holland. It is very likely that Dr. Curtius was one of these refugees.

It must be noted that there was another school of higher education in Kraziai and still another in Koenigsberg, Lithuania Minor. The possibility of his (Curtius) being a professor in either of these schools cannot be excluded. Unfortunately, contemporary records which may have survived wars and foreign invasions are inaccessible due to Soviet Russian occupation of Lithuania.

The possibility of Curtius being an adventurer must be completely excluded. His disputes with burgomasters of New Amsterdam and complaints concerning his salary would tend to show that he was accustomed to a higher standard of living than his income in New Amsterdam could provide.

According to the early records of New York there were 270 inhabitants in 1628, about 700 in 1652, 120 houses and 1,000 souls in 1656, and 200 houses and 1,500 souls in 1659. With the increase in population, the need to establish some kind of school became pressing. There is some evidence that as early as 1638 an elementary school existed in New York with Adam Roelantsen as its school master. Yet in 1647 a schoolhouse as such was still lacking, as is seen from the remark of the Director General of the New Netherland, Peter Stuyvesant: "Whereas for want of a proper place no school has been kept for three months, by which the youth here run wild, it is asked where school can be kept, in order that the youth may be kept from the street and be accustomed to discipline under a pious and diligent schoolmaster."

Governor Stuyvesant must be credited with concern for education, since as early as 1652 he expressed interest in a school above the elementary grades. On September 19, 1658, a new request for a schoolmaster was dispatched to the West India Company directors at Amsterdam. The burgomasters of New Amsterdam hoped that once established the school would eventually become an academy (university). But the obstacle to this plan was the seeming impossibility of funding a sufficiently trained and suitable teacher who would be willing to go to an unexplored and wild land, nor was any person with qualifications to be found in the colony. At long last, the directors of the West India Company at Amsterdam advised Stuyvesant in a letter of April 25, 1659:

"how much trouble we have taken, to find a Latin schoolmaster is shown by the fact, that now one Alexander Carolus Curtius late Professor in Lithuania, goes over, whom we have engaged as such at a yearly salary of 500 fl., board money included; we give him also a present of 100 fl. in merchandise, to be used by him upon his arrival there, as you may learn by the enclosed extract from our resolutions or by the contract, made with him, to which we refer for brevity's sake. Your good friends, The Directors of the W.I. Company, Department of Amsterdam."

Before Curtius arrived, the burgomasters had a schoolhouse built for him on the site a few feet north of what is now the junction of Broad Street and Exchange Place. Dr. Curtius sailed in the Bever on April 25, 1659, and on July 4 appeared before the burgomasters of New Amsterdam. Shortly after arrival, Dr. Curtius opened a Latin school for boys, the highest form of education in New Amsterdam, in the new building.

It was not long before Dr. Curtius began to feel the pinch of high prices in New Amsterdam. He complained to the burgomasters. On September 17, 1659, Sturyvesant wrote to the Directors of the West India Company at Amsterdam:

"The Latin schoolmaster or rector, lately sent over, complains of his salary, because he says it is impossible to support him decently with it, as you may see by his enclosed letter to us. Your repeated instructions do not allow us to raise anybody's salary without your knowledge, we have therefore referred him to you, promising him our favorable recommendation: we now request your Honors' advice, whether a reasonable sum may not be granted to him for board money. As to his services and his diligence, we must truly testify, that his industry is astonishing and the progress of the young people remarkable."

The Directors at Amsterdam appear to have been quite stingy, since in their letter of December 22, 1659, they wrote:

"We believe that the complaints made by the Latin schoolmaster or rector about the insufficiency of his salary are almost answered by the payment of all salaries at Holland valuation, as now ordered, which, with what he receives from his pupils every year should be sufficient to support him decently, as long as he remains a single man; with the increase of the young people in the school his income will increase daily, for the parents of his pupils will not hesitate to remunerate him fairly, if he does his duty."

From further correspondence between the West India Company and Peter Stuyvesant we learn that Dr. Curtius not only taught school but also practiced medicine. In fact, he is considered to have been the first physician of any prominence in New York:

"While the population was creeping up to 1500, which it did not fully reach until 1664, and not long after the arrival of the first schoolmaster, the name of the first physician of any prominence, Alexander C. Curtius, appears. He taught school also...."

The directors of the Company at Amsterdam wrote to Stuyvesant on April 16, 1660:

"As we are told, that Rector Curtius practices medicine there and therefore asked to have a herbarium sent to him, we have been willing to provide him with one herewith, you will hand it to him with the understanding that it shall not cease to be property of the Company, likewise the books sent with and for the above-mentioned clergymen."

Although initially Stuyvesant was delighted with Curtius and recommended to the Amsterdam West India Company that he be given a raise in salary, subsequent misunderstandings between Curtius and the burgomasters and with Stuyvesant led to a complete break and the return of Curtius to Europe in 1661.

On December 27, 1661, Alexander Carolus Curtius "nobilis Lithunus," was matriculated at the University of Leiden, Holland, as "medicinae candidatus." He is listed on page 634 in the Album Inscriptionum, Vol. X, which is in the Archives of the Senate of the University of Leiden. Unfortunately, there is no information about the family background of Dr. Curtius, as is revealed in the letter of the University Library of Leiden of January 6, 1959, wherein it is stated: "It appears that he took his medical degree at Leiden, but that he already was doctor utriusque uris. About his place and date of birth nothing more can be found in our archives."

However, two things remain clear: Dr. Curtius was a professor in Lithuania before coming to New York and he was a Lithuanian nobleman. Lithuanians recognize his name as Latinization of the Lithuanian "Kursius," an inhabitant of Kursas, or of Kurcius, meaning a deaf man. Both these names and their derivatives are still popular among Lithuanians: Kursius, Kursis, Kurselis, Kursaitis, Kursauskas, Kurcius. It is noteworthy that in three of the four documents found in the Documents Relating to the Colonial History of the State of New York his name is spelled Cursius (pages 437, 436, and 443). This may be a simple typographical error, or perhaps Dr. Curtius in the beginning used the Lithuanian form Cursius and changed it later to Curtius. However, his doctoral thesis, "Disputatio Medica Inauguralis, de Calculo Renum ac Vesicae," bears the name Alexander Carolus Curtius, D.

## GENERAL KOSCIUSZKO'S WILL:

## "TO MAKE THEMSELVES HAPPY AS POSSIBLE"

## 1797-1816

Thaddeus Kosciuszko was by far the most celebrated of soldiers who came from the Polish-Lithuanian Commonwealth to fight on the side of the American Revolutionaries during the War of Independence. He returned to the United States in 1797 and prior to leaving drafted a will to have his properties in America used to help free Negroe slaves. This humanitarian will was superceded by others of a later date. Anthony O. Shallna, vice president of the Boston Law Society, traced the adjudication of Kosciuszko's will. His findings follow.

Source: (From A. O. Shallna, "General Kosciuszko - A Lithuanian?" in Anicetas Simutis, Lithuanian World Directory, New York, 1958).

Among the foreign officers in the American Revolutionary War like Lafayette, Von Steuben, and DeKalb, there was a young colonel who landed here in 1776 from Paris with a letter of introduction from Benjamin Franklin to George Washington. In time he became General Washington's aide-de-camp and terminated his services for our country with the rank of Brigadier General. Having received a substantial grant of land and money from Congress, General Thaddeus Kosciuszko before departing for Europe drew a will on May 5, 1798 in which he expressed his humanitarian views:

> I, Thaddeus Kosciuszko, being just on my departure from America, do hereby declare and direct that, should I make no other testamentary disposition of my property in the United States, I hereby authorize my friend Thomas Jefferson to employ the whole thereof in purchasing negroes from his own or any other and giving them liberty in my name; in giving them an education in trade or otherwise; in having them instructed for their new condition in the duties of morality which may make them good neighbors, good fathers, and mothers, husbands and wives, in their duty as citizens; teaching them to be defenders of their liberty and country, of the good order of society, and in whatsoever may make them happy and useful.

....he located in Paris and drew his second will or perhaps a codicil on June 28, 1806. In this will he makes reference to the aims expressed in his first will and he makes a special bequest to Kosciusko Armstrong, a son of his friend General Armstrong. From a photostatic copy of the original will and affidavit of proof, which are historical documents, one may read General Kosciuszko's fondest thoughts and history correcting data, namely:

> Know all men by these presents that I Thaedo Kosciusko formerly an officer of the United States of America in their Revolutionary War against Great Britain, and a native of Lithuania in Poland, at present residing at Paris, do hereby will and direct that at my decease the sume of Three thousand seven hundred and four dollars currency of the aforesaid United States shall of right be possessed by and delivered over to the full enjoyment and use of Kosciusko Armstrong the son of General John Armstrong Minister Plenipotentiary of said States at Paris, for the security and performance whereof, I do hereby instruct and authorize my only lawful Executor in the said United States, Thomas Jefferson President thereof to reserve in trust for that special purpose, of the Funds he already holds belonging to me, the aforesaid sum of Three thousand seven hundred and four dollars in principal to be paid by him the said Thomas Jefferson immediately after my decease, to him the aforesaid Kosciusko Armstrong and in case of his death to the use and benefit of his surviving Brothers.
>
> Given under my hand and seal at Paris this twenty eighth day of June One thousand eight hundred and six.
>
> (Signature) Thade Kosciuszko
> In presence of
> Charles Carter
> James M. Morris.

<u>Commercial Agency of the United States - Paris</u>

On this twenty-eighth day of June in the year of our Lord one thousand eight hundred and six and of the independence of the United States of America the thirtieth, before the undersigned, commercial agent and Agent of Prize-Causes for the United States of America at Paris, personally appeared Thade' Koscouszko, late officer of the said United States, who in his presence signed and sealed the foregoing Transfer in favor of Kosciuszko Armstrong, the son of General John Armstrong, Minister Plenipotentiary of the United States at Paris, and in case of his Death to the use and benefit of his surviving Brothers, and did acknowledge it as his own act and deed for the purpose therein specified. --

In testimony whereof he the said undersigned as aforesaid has hereunto signed his name and affixed his seal of office at Paris the day and year above written.

(Signature) Fulwar Skipwith

District of Columbia
Washington County, to Wit:
The 19th day of November,
---James M. Morris, one of the subscribing witnesses to the aforegoing instrument of writing, purporting to be the last

will and testament of Thadeus Kosciuszko, deceased, made oath on the Holy Evangels of Almighty God, that he did see the testator therein named sign that this will -- that he published, pronounced and declared the same to be his last will and testament -- that, at the time of his so doing, he was to the best of his apprehensions, of sound and disposing mind, memory and understanding -- and, that he, together with Charles Carter, the other subscribing witness, respectively subscribed their names as witnesses to this will, in the presence and at the request of the testator, and in the presence of each other. --

Sworn in open court.

(Signed) Test. Henry C. Neale, Rg. Wills.

On June 4, 1816 Kosciuszko drew a holographic will as his third will, apparently revoking the prior wills. In this will made at Soleure, Switzerland, he used this language: "I, the undersigned Thaddeus Kosciuszko, residing at Berville, in the township of Genevrage, of the Department of Seine and Marne, (being now) or at present at Soleure, in Switzerland."

His fourth will was drawn October 10, 1817, and in this will nothing is said of his residence.

General Kosciuszko was more than a good general. He was an outstanding humanitarian - a forerunner of the abolishment of slavery. He preceded President Abraham Lincoln by about sixty-five years in taking steps to abolish slavery both in this country and in Europe.

Biographers, historians and others who have tried to present General Kosciuszko to us have made use of his will of 1798 but have not even made a reference to his second and other wills. Any degree of research should have brought forth the existence of these other wills. It was the will of 1806 that was analyzed and substantiated by our Supreme Court.

The record in the administration of Kosciuszko's estate has been correct but not all of us have been apprized of it. Since this case had been considered at length by the United States Supreme Court and the documents and proofs in this cause from the Orphans' Court, the genealogy of the Kosciuszko family and the collateral relatives of the persons entitled to a decree, and also the wills of Kosciuszko are properly in evidence in this suit and the record from Grodno (Gardinas) is judicial, not a judgment _inter partes_, but a foreign judgment _in rem_, "which is evidence of the facts adjudicated against all the world," we might state the essential and interesting parts of the Court's opinion.

With the will of 1816 revoking the wills of 1798 and 1806 and no disposition having been made in it or in the will of 1817 of the Funds in controversy, as to which General Kosciuszko died intestate, it became necessary to find out which relatives may be entitled to inherit from him according to the law of his domicil at the time of his death.

In proceeding to the question of domicil the Court said, "In the will of 1806 he describes himself as 'an officer of the United States of America in their Revolutionary War against Great Britain, and a native of Lithuania in Poland, at present residing in Paris.'"

In the will of 1816 he refers to his residence in Switzerland. And in the will of 1817 nothing is said as to his residence. There was no proof that he was not in France continuously until 1815 when he went to Vienna.

The Court also observed that "Kosciuszko's domicil or origin was Lithuania in Poland." The presumption of law is that the domicil was retained unless the change is proved and the burden of proving it is upon him who alleges the change. The Court ruled that from his own declarations and other proofs in the record that he was domiciled in France at the time of his death.

The Court then ordered, adjudged and decreed that the legal domicil at the time of his death in 1817 was in France; that the will of October 10, 1817, had not disposed of the Funds in this country; that the Fund in this country is to be distributed according to the law of France, the place of his domicil at the time of his death, and that the estate belongs to his lineal descendents, that is to two sisters of Kosciuszko's cousin.

## A HERO OF THE CIVIL WAR:

## CAPTAIN ALEXANDER BIELASKI

## 1861

When the American Civil War broke out, the handful of Lithuanians, especially the exile rebels of the 1831 Revolt, identified with the Union and were opposed to slavery. Alexander Beleckas or Bielaski as he was called by Americans died a heroe's death on November 7, 1861 during the battle of Belmont, Missouri. A friend, John Gilmary Shea, included a brief biography of this valiant Lithuanian soldier in his second volume of "A Child's History of the United States" (1879)

Source: John Gilmary Shea, "Alexander Bielaski," A Child's History of the United States, Volume II, New York, 1872, pp. 408-415.

On the bank of a small lake in the Grand Ducy of Lithuania, on the 1st day of August 1811, Alexander Bielaski was born. At the proper age he was sent to a military academy, where he received his education as a topographical engineer for the Russian Army. In 1831, Poland determined to shake off the yoke of Russian vassalage, and broke out into revolution. Bielaski, then about 20, engaged with ardent zeal in the cause of his country....

In 1832, he quit France, and came to America. He landed at Portland, Maine, and very soon obtained employment as engineer upon a railroad.

At this time he was totally ignorant of the English language, but he had some knowledge of the French, by means of which he managed to make himself understood until he learned by the ear as much of our tongue as sufficed for the ordinary exigencies of life. In after years, he became quite proficient in the use of English.

In 1835 he went to Florida on a surveying expedition, which carried him into various perils and difficulties. Ever ready to brave danger, he took the lead whenever there appeared ought to dread, and with the same stirring cry which he uttered in his last daring charge, "Follow me," he would dash into swamps, swarming with alligators, or thickets alive with Seminoles, his very fearlessness seeming to be his safety.

From Florida, he went, in the year 1837, to Illinois, and engaged as engineer on the Illinois Central Railroad, under the well-known engineer and contractor Arthur Hoyt. Here he was occupied in the most laborious duties of the profession; and such was his energy and power of endurance, that often when his assistants, completely worn out, could go no further, he would load himself with their baggage, adding all the chain and compass, and thus encumbered would return to their camp and send back horses for his exhausted comrades. It was while engaged upon this work that he was attacked by ague and fever, the common disease of that country. He felt that his time was too valuable to be wasted in waiting for the slow process of cure in ordinary practice, so he took a whole box of patent pills at one dose, and, when the chill came on, swallowed a tumblerful of pure brandy. He admitted that the remedies would probably have caused death in any other man, but he never had another chill.

He became a citizen of the United States in June 1841, and on the 17th of July 1842 he was married to Miss Mary Ann Carey, of Springfield, Illinois. In the following November, he went to the city of Mexico, where he was immediately employed as an engineer. During his residence in that country, he was constantly engaged; sometimes for the Government, sometimes for private individuals; but always for a very handsome salary. In March 1843, he received from Santa Anna papers of naturalization, accompanied by the offer of a high rank in the Mexican Army. This offer was wisely declined, and after remaining eighteen months in Mexico, he returned to Illinois, where he devoted two years to farming. On the list of September 1845, he was appointed to a clerkship in the General Land Office, by General Shields, who at that time was a commissioner. In this post, his talents as a draftsman were often brought into requisition, and after a time procured him the place of assistant draftsman.

After passing more than eight years in the faithful performance of these peaceful duties, Bielaski's warrior spirit was again roused. President Lincoln had known him intimately while a resident in Illinois and highly appreciated his military capacity. Soon after the commencement of the present war, the president offered him a commission as captain in the regular army, and Bielaski immediately accepted. Upon entering the service he was attached to the staff of General McClernand and ordered to Cairo. He delayed only long enough to take his family back to their old home in Springfield, Illinois, and then hastened to join the division to which he belonged. The first engagement in which they took part was the Battle of Belmont, which was fought on the 7th of November 1861. Bielaski's horse was shot from under him, and while advancing on foot, with the flag of his adopted country in his hand, shouting to the soldiers to follow him he fell, instantly killed by a cannonball. General McClernand made many efforts to regain his body, but it had been buried with a mass of other dead, and could not be recovered.

Captain Bielaski was about 5 feet and 8 inches high, broad shouldered, and well formed for strength and endurance, rather than for grace and activity. His face, though disfigured by a shot, was pleasing to look upon, especially when graphically describing some hard-fought battle. Then his gray eyes sparkled with excitement, and the veins in his high, broad forehead would swell as the battle thickened. He was always frank and openhearted, sometimes blunt, but never offensive. He was the soul of truth. His promise to do a thing was, to all who knew him an assurance that it would be done.

He has fallen for his adopted country - may that country never forget him.

## FINDING WORK IN THE NEW COUNTRY

1884

Dr. Jonas Sliupas, the controversial civic leader and activist of the Lithuanian National Renaissance Movement in Lithuania and America, left an account of the trials and hardships of trying to earn a living in a strange country.

Source: Stasys Michelsonas, "Jonas Sliupas," Lietuviu Iseivija Amerikoje, South Boston, Keleivis Press, 1961, p. 398.

I did not come to his country the way present day emigrants go. I was driven out of my homeland. I had no choice but to row across the ocean or go to jail or, worse yet, to Siberia. I did not believe that I would find sweet cakes here (in America). But what I did encounter here, did surprise me.... In 1884 I landed in America, alone, not knowing the language, friendless and without acquaintances. To make matters worse, I did not have any money. I did not have a trade. Where to go? I went to an office which provided work for immigrants. There it was suggested that I drive out to the farm country. I immediately agreed. It was my luck to work during the hot month of July. Unaccustomed to hard physical labor, I suffer. That's not all. I have to milk the cows. The cows here are milked in a peculiar manner - with the entire hand. Of course, I was not familiar with this work. That is why I was given a shovel. Everything would have been all right but for the fact that I had soft, though big hands which were not used to grasping hard things. Terrible blisters appeared: on one palm and fingers I was able to count 24 sores, on the other hand - 25. I was unable to bend my fingers, oh how the pain was unspeakable!...

I did not endure for long. Dropping this job I walked several miles on foot, carrying my kit on my back, like the Jewish tradesman in Lithuania, and found myself on the outskirts of Newbourgh. After a few days rest, I went to work in a brickyard. This work ruined my hands even more. I dropped the job and walked to New York City, where I was determined to acquire a trade. And in truth I entered a barber shop where I learned a skill. Later I opened by own barbershop ("balbierne") with a half-Lithuanian as partner....

## THE FOUNDING OF ST. GEORGE LITHUANIAN PARISH

## 1891

The vast majority of Lithuanian immigrants were religiously devote peasants. If asked of their nationality, many would naively reply, "Roman Catholics!" At first the Lithuanians joined with Poles and Slovaks in forming Roman Catholic parishes. Gradually, through the efforts of patriotic priests, such as Alexander Burba, they founded their own churches with services and confessions in the native Lithuanian tongue. The founding of St. George's Church in Shenandoah, Pennsylvania is the prototype of similar efforts in scores of communities during the eighteen nineties.

Source: Antanas Kucas, St. George's Parish Shenandoah, Pa., Brooklyn, New York, Franciscan Fathers Press, 1968, pp. 179-183.

The predominant desire of the Lithuanians was to establish their own parish. For that purpose they solicited funds. They sent delegations to Archbishop Ryan in an effort to convince him that a Lithuanian parish was necessary, and that they were capable of having a church erected, but their pleas fell on deaf ears. He was doubtful of their ability, since the first solicitor of funds vanished with all the money. But he changed his opinion when Father Abromaitis appeared on the scene, and to whom he granted permission to organize a parish in Mahanoy City. Father Abromaitis was no stranger to Shenandoah, for he used to come there to conduct services for the Lithuanians and to hear their confessions.

Despite the many instigations and humiliations caused by the Poles and atheists,...some brave and determined men were found among the Lithuanians. On February 12, 1891, eighteen such men called a secret meeting in which they decided to finally separate themselves from the mixed Lithuanian-Polish St. Casimir's parish, and, in spite of everything, to organize a new Lithuanian parish. To back up their words, J. Bobinas, J. Mieldazis, the Miliauskas brothers, Casimir Radzavage and J. Razas each contributed $100; V. Chmieliauskas, S. Mockaitis, J. Skritulskas and T. Satrinskas $50 each; T. Astramskas $15; others donated less. St. George Society gave $500; St. Peter Society $150; and the Algirdas Society contributed $50.

This effort was crowned with success. Archbishop Patrick J. Ryan of Philadelphia finally permitted the Lithuanians to establish their own parish, to which he assigned Father Peter Abromaitis as pastor. On March 31, 1891, a general meeting of all Lithuanians was convened in Robbin's Hall. About 1500 persons were present.

Father Abromaitis officially announced that permission was given to organize a Lithuanian parish. His words were greeted with great enthusiasm. Immediately elected was a committee of 13 men, together with 21 solicitors who would appeal for funds toward the erection of a new church.

The name of the new parish was that of St. George, because the St. George Society was largely instrumental in founding the parish...St. George...is depicted as riding on a white charger with a spear raised to strike a dragon. He symbolized the victory of good over evil. No one could deny that this name or symbol was very appropriate to the Shenandoah Lithuanians.

During that same meeting a substantial sum of money was raised toward the erection of a new church. Up to April 27, 1891, more than $4,000 was contributed. All this adversely affected Father Lenarikiewicz of St. Casimir's Church, who could not understand how the Lithuanians obtained the Archbishop's permission to organize the new parish. Now he became more furious toward the Lithuanians. "He (Father Lenarkiewicz) has become so angry that no one dares to approach him; if any one comes to see him he drives them away with a cane. On Holy Saturday he refused to give holy water to Lithuanians, telling them to go to their own priest. If any one is dying, he refuses to visit the sick." His organist D. T. Backauskas, and other Lithuanian rascals, called "the new Poles," imitated his example. They explained to all who would listen that in Shenandoah one church was sufficient, namely, St. Casimir Church. They added there was no reason to burden the people with such a heavy debt; furthermore, the brotherly bonds between Lithuanians and Poles were being severed. John Sliupas, who had recently arrived in Shenandoah (1888), also advanced the same arguments. He asserted that the work of the Lithuanians in founding their parish was akin to giving their money to the Irish Bishop.

Such criticism, however, did not daunt the Lithuanians of good will. Soon three parcels of land were purchased at the corner of South Jardin and Cherry Streets. The three lots totalled 13,500 square feet and cost $6,000. Before long three acres of land for a cemetery were acquired along the Ringtown road. Before the land was purchased, the Archbishop's consent was obtained and this property of the Lithuanian parish was registered in the Schuylkill County Recorder of Deeds Office (Deed Book #225, p. 550, Archbishop P. J. Ryan). The persevering Lithuanians overcame many obstacles. The false assertions of their foes and their faint-hearted brethren had gone with the wind. Now a happy day dawned - the blessing of the cornerstone of St. George Church. The Lithuanians invited their friends and neighbors to the ceremony. October 26, 1891 was a bright and beautiful day. Father F. H. O'Reilly, of the local Annunciation Parish was delegated by the Archbishop to perform the ceremony. About 5,000 people attended the auspicious event. Lithuanians and those of other nationalities were present. Many people arrived from other towns in Pennsylvania, such as Plymouth, Pittston, Hazleton, Freeland, Mahanoy City, Girardville, Ashland, Mahanoy Plane, Lost Creek, Shamokin, Mt. Carmel and St. Clair. Among the clergy were Father Alexander Burba, Plymouth; Reverend Simon Pautienius, Baltimore, Maryland; Reverend Joseph Zlotozinskas, Pittston, Reverend Schuttlehoefler of the local German Holy Family Parish; and Father Peter Abromaitis of Mahanoy City. Father Lenarkiewicz was conspicuous by his absence.

Among the people were many members of local and distant organizations. Most of them were in uniform and they carried flags and banners. After the ceremony a huge parade advanced along the streets. Two bands also participated, and they drew much attention. Shenandoahans for the first time saw how many Lithuanians lived here and how beautifully they arranged things in an orderly manner. It was like a national Lithuanian holiday, a victory celebration, a public demonstration of Lithuanian unity and power.

Soon after the ceremony, the construction of the new church began. The contractor, J. W. Johnson, had promised to build the church in one year, but the job took a much longer time. The parishioners themselves almost completed the work. In place of contributing their annual dues to the church and paying an assessment of $21.25 toward the building fund, they went to work on the project counting each day's work equivalent to $1.25. Therefore, having worked 17 days, they were considered true members of the parish and they were exonerated from paying their dues for one full year. As soon as the basement of the church was completed, an altar was set up and Mass was offered. The church itself was a wooden structure, but later it was covered with tin and painted to simulate stone. It was 120 feet long and 56 feet wide. The seating capacity was 800. The interior of the church was artistically painted in light and soothing colors. The windows were of stained glass containing pictures of saints.

The dedication ceremonies took place on May 12, 1894 and attraced many people. A young priest, Father John Zilinskas of Mt. Carmel, was invited to preach the dedication sermon. He praised the work of the parishioners and the beauty of the church, comparing its beauty with the greater beauty of God's world. He urged all to be united as parishioners, just as the created world is united in harmony.

Hardly had the church been completed when a severe storm toppled two of its wooden towers or steeples. The parishioners blamed the contractor for this incident and they took the case to court. The trial consumed a considerable sum of money, but the parishioners failed to win the case. Adjoining the church, a rectory was built. It cost $10,000, and, with a few improvements it was used to this very day. The basement of the church was partitioned to provide a parish school, in which the organist taught reading, writing and religion; a large meeting room; and a hall for social events. At that time the parish property was valued at $125,000 and it was debt free.

In a comparatively short time the parish consisted of 1200 families and 2500 individuals. About 5,000 persons used to fulfill their Easter duty. Each year there was an average of 120 weddings, 500 baptisms and 400 funerals. The annual income averaged over $10,000. To assist the pastor in his administrative duties, each year the parishioners elected a committee consisting of a president, secretary, treasurer and twelve other members. From the parish treasury were paid the salaries of the rector, organist, sacristan and teacher and also all parish and church bills. Each month the committee members held a regular meeting, and every three months they gave a financial report. All checks were signed by the president, secretary and treasurer. When the parish was established, Father P. Abromaitis held the office of treasurer for twelve consecutive years.

While the parish was being established, a group of people suggested that in seeking a charter, all parish property should be registered not in the name of the Bishop, but in the name of the parish. The Archbishop, however, did not approve of their plan because the parish was not yet free of debt. He gave a loan of $5,000 to the parish and at a meeting held on June 21, 1891, the parishioners voted to register all parish property in the name of the Archbishop of Philadelphia....That loan was repaid by Father J. A. Karalius in 1940.

# THE MASSACRE OF COALMINERS AT LATTIMER, PENNSYLVANIA

# 1897

The working conditions and lot of 19th century eastern and southern European immigrants were atrocious. Exploited by the mine owners and company stores, risking life and limb in damp and perilous excavations, the wretched mine-workers began to organize and demand safer working conditions and decent wages. Concomitant with labor organization came the only effective weapon of labor - the strike. The mine-owners often retaliated with the lockout and more drastically with armed suppression. The "Massacre of Mine-workers" in the Pennsylvania town of Lattimer is a bitter memory in the history of the Lithuanians in America. The socialist Lithuanian-language newspaperman Stasys Michelsonas has left us a graphic account based on contemporary Lithuanian accounts.

Source: A. Milukas, Amerikos Lietuviai XIX Simtmetyje, Philadelphia, 1938, pp. 152-173.

...In 1890 the United Mine Workers of America were formed, unifying all of the individual coalminer unions in the east. The Lithuanian sources of the era state that quite a few Lithuanian coalminers were active in the formation of these labor organizations. Some were even referred to as "Lithuanian unions" (lietuviskos unijos). Rev. J. Zilinskas in his book Amerikos Lietuviai XIX Simtmetyje maintains that the Lithuanian miners of the environs of Shenandoah, Pa. were agitating for "consolidation of all coalminers of all nationalisties." According to Rev. Milukas, the Lithuanian coalminers union of Shenandoah, Pa., had 4,000 members when it joined the United Mine Workers of America.

In 1897 this coalminers organization declared a strike in which some 150,000 workers participated in, although "The Encyclopedia of Social Sciences" writes that the numbers did not exceed 10,000 members of the UMWA.

The mines were worked in the main by immigrants: Lithuanians, Poles, Slovaks and Italians. Despite the fact that 150,000 workers went on strike, some mines continued operations. Among the mines not observing the strikers' declaration was the Lattimer Mine in Luzerne County, some five miles from the hamlet of Hazleton. Therefore, on September 10, 1897, some 500 striking mine workers assembled and decided to march to Lattimer and call upon the local miners to join the strike. As they marched along the highway, their path was blocked by the sheriff of Luzerne County with a hundred deputies. The marching strikers topped at a distance. The sheriff approached them, grasping a revolver in each hand. He told them to go back. Several young men, conversant in English, began to explain that the strikers were marching peacefully without any weapons and that they did not intend to do any harm to anyone. Therefore, why could they not continue on their way? The sheriff raised one hand to pistol-whip one of the young men; the latter instinctively blocked the sheriff's hand and the revolver fell from his hand. Thereupon the sheriff read the "act of riot" and ordered his deputies to open fire. A shot was heard, followed by a second, and then there was a thunderous volley. Some people immediately fell, others began to scatter. The sheriff and his hirelings fired upon the fleeing miners. They fired in pursuit.

When the shooting subsided, there were 21 corpses on the ground and 55 wounded strikers. The local people came to aid the wounded, carrying them to their homes, while the sheriff's hirelings lit cigars and mocked the carnage.

Among the slain were the following Lithuanians: Antanas Grikis from Simnas parish; Jonas Tarnavicius from Lazdijai parish; Pranas Keidelis from Veisejai parish; Jokubas Tamosiunas and Rapolas Rakevicius, both from the district of Vilnius.

Universal revulsion and protests against this massacre were expressed by the workers organizations and the press. There were demands that the sheriff and his hirelings be drawn into court. In truth, litigation was initiated, but only for the exonoration of the killers. The trial was a case of whitewash.

....After the Lattimer Massacre the coalminers realized that they needed greater unity and a stronger organization. After this unfortunate incident the United Mine Workers grew into a giant organization. All of the Lithuanian coalminers joined them. The following Lithuanian miners unions joined the UMWA: Shenandoah - 4,000 members; Mahanoy City - 2,000; Hazleton - 500. There were "Lithuanian unions" in other Pennsylvania towns as well: Shamokin, Gilberton, Plymouth, Mt. Carmel, Lost Creek, etc. The Lithuanian miners union of Westville, Illinois, had 515 members and donated $400 to the Tevynes Myletoju Draugija to publish a book about the hardships of the coalminers.

Although the workers in the mines were not as exploited as those in factories, their work was dangerous. Going to work in the morning, the coalminer was not sure that he would come home that night or that he might not be carted back to the family a corpse. Scarcely a day went by, when someone was not killed or injured in the mine. For example, in 1897 in the Shenandoah mines 41 Lithuanians were killed, 5 in Mt. Carmel, 6 in the vicinity of Throop, Pennsylvania. This does not acccunt for the injured. In the Cherry mine of Illinois an explosion took place in 1909 which took 384 miners' lives, among them were 23 Lithuanians.

## THE EARLY IMMIGRANTS IN PENNSYLVANIA

## 1899

Jr. Jonas (Reverend Jonas Zilinskas), publicist and editor of numerous Lithuanian newspapers, was the first historian of the social and cultural life of the Lithuanian immigrants in America. In 1899 he wrote an extensive series of articles, entitled "Lietuviai Amerikoj" (Lithuanians in America), which first appeared in the Lithuanian Alliance organ Tevyne and later in book form in 1899. The early Lithuanian immigrants led a boisterous and hard life, which is graphically portrayed in the excerpts below.

Source: Jr. Jonas, "Lietuviai Amerikoj," Tevyne, IV, No. 10-11, Plymouth, Pennsylvania, October and November, 1899, pp. 354-357, 401-403.

...It is not easy to change the character of a person; old customs are the secondary elements of a person's character. Some of our writers call the Lithuanians conservative, but I claim that no other nation is able to unite with foreign elements as quickly as the Lithuanians. Among the Chinese in America rare is the individual who will give up wearing his "sandals"; the Arabs hawk their wares in the same manner as their brothers back home; the Italians are not ashamed to continue to wear velvet caps and vests. Hungarian women after a dozen years here still wear their traditional shawls... But the Lithuanians residing in the great cities want to adapt American habits quickly. If they learn the tongue, they try to pretend that they are native Americans. That's a fact.

Their (Lithuanian) parties, christenings, weddings, funerals, etc., though retaining their Lithuanian character, have adopted, to a large degree, the milder, more restrained American manner of social activities. The parties become shorter, less riotous. At the same time, in the Pennsylvania coalmining regions and in the small towns the Lithuanians still try to observe the above-mentioned social functions in the so-called Lithuanian fashion. The wedding lasts for two or three days, as in Lithuania, with continuous dancing and drinking. Fights break out among the drunken guests. There are even killings. Thus, for example, since the founding of the Mt. Carmel Parish, that is, between 1892 and 1897, there were two murders during wedding festivities. During the wedding reception, the Lithuanians would dance their own unique steps. In more polite homes, where non-Lithuanians would also attend, there was changing of partners and even party games. The bride and her maids of honor would oft wear a twig of rue, a custom unknown to the Yankees. The wedding party rarely went to church on foot. They always went by carriage. If necessary the bridal party would rent out carriages for the occasion. In the old days, the Lithuanians would collect gifts for the married couple. From two to three hundred dollars would be collected for the young couple. Though this custom has survived to this day, the size of the gift is not as great. Even in Pennsylvania the boisterous wedding festivities have begun to subside. During Irish wakes and funerals the people smoke pipes: they purchase several pounds of tobacco, a few dozen pipes at a cent a pipe and smoke through the wake in order to stay awake. Our people are somewhat more respectful; following old country customs they sing hymns. The only problem is that the drunken mourners might sing a bit too loudly and keep the neighbors awake.

In the large cities the Lithuanians are more cultured and during the wakes they rarely sing hymns aloud.

A Lithuanian, who has belonged to a benefit society, is buried with pomp; his friends attend to his coffin in church and at the cemetery resplendid in their societal uniforms.

In order to get married, that is, to hold a boisterous wedding, the Lithuanian American must expend quite a bit of cash. First of all, if the bride is a newcomer from Lithuania, a grinorka (greenhorn), the groom-to-be must buy her attire, shoes and dreses (dresses), two golden rings. The groom must pay for the wedding, if he wants a mass. A wedding with a mass costs from fiteen to twenty dollars, while the marriage ceremony without a mass costs from $5 to $10. The "skvajeris" or justice of the peace charges five dollars for a non-religious ceremony. However, these civil ceremonies are a rarity among the Lithuanians. Red Socialists go for civil ceremonies. In addition, the carriage to and from the marriage ceremony costs three to five dollars. Add to this the musicians, the food and especially the liquor and the entire wedding costs the newly-weds from $100 to $150. Those who do not hold wedding parties get by with $50 and even with $20.

Ordinarily, a funeral costs upwards of one hundred dollars. When a person dies, the undertaker (graborius) is solicited. He brings an "ice box", that is, a box with ice wherein the corpse is placed and carted to the funeral parlor. During the burial the undertaker uses a lacquered coffin or one with a black velvet interior. He uses a hearst with a pair of black or grey horses. For this the family must pay $40 to $60, at times even a hundred or several hundred dollars, depending on the luxury of the funeral. If the funeral Mass is solicited, then another ten to twenty five dollars must be laid out. Rarely is the one dollar ceremony without Mass solicited.

In the case of poor or invalid Lithuanians, at times relatives, acquaintances, friends and compatriots would put together a donation to assist decent folk in defraying the cost of burial. Priests would perform their services free of charge for needy decent folk.....

One need not write much about christenings. Suffice it to say, that most baptisms in American Catholic churches take place on Sundays after the masses; the godparents pay for the baptism in the amount of $3-$5. Lithuanians do not hold boisterous christening parties.

The greatest social activites are the balls or dances. Parishes and societies hold dances. So do clubs, local chapters or other kinds of organizations. Lithuanians do not organize dances as individuals. The society would hire a hall for an affair. The cost of the hall would run from $10 to $60 per evening or night. Deciding to hold a social, the society would carry an ad in the Lithuanian newspapers and would print placards. The tickets to the social would cost between 25 and 50 cents a person. Most often women would not pay for admission. Food and drink would be sold separately. This would be the source of profit for the organization holding the affair. In olden times when Lithuanian dances were rarely held, the profit would amount to $200, $300 and $500. At present, the profits are rather small. The amusements would take the form of music, dancing, social chatting and "socializing." Drunkards would have a field day, for there would be no limit to the amount of liquor they could consume at these functions. These dances would begin at 6 or 7 p.m. and last till 5 a.m. the next morning. Certain jurisdictions in the United States prohibit the sale of alcoholic beverages at dances. At these functions carbonated drinks would be served. Such functions would play English dances.

Another form of social amusement in this country is the picnic or piknikas which, like the dance, is organized by societies which would rent a place in the country or woods for an outdoor function. Outside of cities are special picnic grounds with dance floors, benches and picnic tables. Like the dances, food, drink and music is offered. In general, dances or parties are held during the winter months, while picnics are sponsored in the summer.

Excursions or, to use the Lithuanian vernacular, pasivazinejimai, are at times sponsored by the parishes. The trip would last the entire day with a special picnic during the pause in an attractive locale.

Such social functions are held by societies and parishes as a form of organizational "business."

The traditional forms of amusement of the Lithuanian worker in America are concerts, songfests, speeches. Concerts are held by Lithuanian bands. These bands are almost exclusively formed of wind instruments. There are few Lithuanians who would play other types of instruments. Aside from concerts, the Lithuanian bands would be hired out to play for various ceremonies and functions when the societies would assemble in colorful uniforms, as during the consecration of churches, the opening of the Lithuanian Alliance conventions, and special expositions, or dances and picnics. Amateurs would organize theatrical performances. These amateurs would organize theatrical societies or troupes. In recent years, as stated in the chronicles of the Lithuanian language newspapers, our people have taken a liking to theatrics and are performing more plays. One has to wonder at the efforts of ordinary workers who take up play-acting. Songfests are held by organists after speech-making. Church choirs or children's chorales would sing. Amateur soloists would also appear. Speeches were delivered by speakers, who, to be frank, are not very numerous among our immigration in America. However, there are more and more speeches as the art of eloquition is developing among our people.

Among the amusements of our immigrants one must list evenings and Sundays spent in reading books and good newspapers. Yet one is forced to admit that our reading public in the United States is still relatively small. Rowdies and drifters spend their time in saloons "saliunai" drinking, fighting, mocking, ridiculing, gossiping, cussing, and even, God Forbid, drawing blood. These uncouth undertakings are considered as amusements by our rude element....

These rowdy outbursts lead to arrests, litigation and the lowering of Lithuanian prestige among non-Lithuanians. It is difficult to cite statistics here, yet a perusal of the records of the records of the Pottsville and Wilkes Barre courts, for example, will show that no other nationality has had its sons go to court over such petty outbursts as have our Lithuanian lads. Revenge is an inherent Lithuanian trait, which has cost the Lithuanian in America a lot of money. There is an expression in Pennsylvania: "skvajerai ir sudzios lietuviszkas (ir abelnai svetimtautiszkas) bylas nesudija kitaip, kaip tik liepdami uzsimoketi pusiau kasztus." (That is: the magistrates and courts do not decide Lithuanian and (foreign) cases in any other manner than half court costs."

...Like other immigrants, the Lithuanians began to form mutual aid societies in this country...Thus, a member would pay 50 cents a month in dues to the society, and if he became sick he would receive a sickness benefit (ligoj paszelpa) of five dollars a week. The member who becomes severely ill is visited and cared for, day and night, by two fellow members. When a member dies, in addition to paying for the burial expenses, the other members would contribute a dollar apiece to help the deceased member's widow, children and parents. Mutual benefit societies are important charitable institutions. The majority of Lithuanians join two and even three such societies.

In addition to sickness and death benefits, these societies have other aims: fraternal activities, temperance, patriotic endeavors...The so-called soldiers societies (kareiviszkos draugystes), in addition to charity, boast of the fact that during special occasions, the members wear "military" uniforms. Political societies engage in politics during elections.

The mutual benefit societies of the other nationalities are united in alliances, which number several thousand or even upwards of twenty thousand members. The Poles have five or six such alliances, the Slovaks have three, the Ruthenians two, the Magyars two. Our own Lithuanians are spoiled ("dideliai iszpaikinti"), they only have one organization, The Lithuanian National Alliance. This Alliance has united only several benefit societies, the majority of members are formed in kuopos or lodges. It is understandable the alliances of the other nationalities, based on mutual aid societies, are stronger than our own Alliance and grow rapidly. Our biggest deterent to growth is the fact that political factions are in conflict within the Alliance, and this frightens potential members away.

The purpose of alliances is to provide members with life insurance. Our own Alliance offers in addition to insurance cultural and patriotic activities. Since our Alliance offers relatively low amounts of insurance many Lithuanians join the Polish National

Alliance, which offers large amounts of insurance.

...according to an old tradition, the Lithuanians fraternized with the Poles. In truth, I know many compatriots, who did not speak a word of Polish when they arrived in America, however, by associating with Poles and Slovaks at work, in the Polish parishes and societies, came to speak a tolerable Polish jargon. Other Lithuanians even learned Slovak. As far as learning English is concerned, as I have said before, the Lithuanians have great difficulty in learning the language. Of the old immigrants, very few learned to read English. It was a great rarety to find Lithuanians who could write in English. In business and in most transactions with non-Lithuanians, it is the young generation which comes to the aid of their parents. Those Lithuanians, who plan to return to the homeland, ignore the language completely, saying that for the time being they can get along without it.

Nonetheless, as with habits and customs, the language of the native Americans has made a great impact on the vocabulary of the Lithuanian immigrants. On the third day after his arrival in this country, the Lithuanian says "yes" in English, instead of the Lithuanian "taip." He will answer "no" in English, instead of "ne," and "gudbay" instead of "Su Diev!" Many English expressions and words have entered his everyday speech....

The number of English and American loanwords is copious. On the other hand, the Lithuanian language is being refined here in America. Many of the immigrants are improving their language skills by reading Lithuanian-language newspapers which are standardizing the language. Thus, a Samogitian after several years in America no longer speaks "Zemaitiskai"; a Kapsas no longer speaks his dialect, a Dzukas ceases to use his dialect. All of these speakers use one uniform language - Lithuanian. This language is beginning to approximate the literary language being developed in the homeland.

One must say that Lithuanian literature in America is flourishing.

The Prussian and Moscovite governments are systematically persecuting Lithuanianism in Lithuania Proper and East Prussia. The Lithuanian movement has found a haven here in America. Serious newspapers are being published here in America. The number of books published is continually increasing. Many energetic young Lithuanian intellectuals, fleeing from tsarist oppression, are coming to these shores. Their ardour has inspired the earlier immigrants. This phenomenon would require a separate study for which I do not have the time at present....

## THE LITHUANIANS IN UPTON SINCLAIR'S THE JUNGLE:

## A LITHUANIAN WEDDING IN CHICAGO

## 1900

In some of the most harrowing scenes ever written in modern literature, the realistic novelist Upton Sinclair depicts factory life in Chicago in the first years of this century. The horrors of the slaughter houses, their atrocious working conditions, the despair - all are revealed through the eyes of the Lithuanian immigrant Jurgis Rudkus, his fiancee and her family. Upton Sinclair shows sociological insight into the mentality of the Lithuanian immigrants of that era. He also captures the folk mores and customs of Lithuanians, and even displays a rudimentary knowledge of the language. Social historians should pay especial attention to the graphic and true description Mr. Sinclair gives of a Lithuanian old-style wedding.

...When the song is over, it is time for the speech, and old Dede Antanas rises to his feet...

Generally it is the custom for the speech at a veselija to be taken out of one of the books and learned by heart, but in his youthful days Dede Antanas used to be a scholar, and really made up all the love letters of his friends. Now it is understood that he has composed an original speech of congratulation and benediction, and this is one of the events of the day. Even the boys, who are romping about the room, draw near and listen, and some of the women sob and wipe their aprons in their eyes. It is very solemn, for Antanas Rudkus has become possessed of the idea that he has not much longer to stay with his children. His speech leaves them all so tearful that one of the guests, Jokubas Szedvilas, who keeps a delicatessen store on Halsted Street, and is fat and hearty, is moved to rise and say that things may not be as bad as that, and then to go on and make a little speech of his own, in which he showers congratulations and prophecies of happiness upon the bride and groom, proceeding to particulars which greatly delight the young men, but which cause Ona to blush more furiously than ever. Jokubas possesses what his wife complacently describes as poetiszka vaidintuve - a poetical imagination.

Now a good many of the guests have finished, and, since there is no pretense of ceremony, the banquet begins to break up. Some of the men gather about the bar; some wander about, laughing and singing; but here and there will be a little group, chanting merrily, and in sublime indifference to the others and to the orchestra as well. Everybody is more of less restless - one would guess that something is on their minds. And so it proves. The last tardy diners are scarcely given time to finish, before the tables and debris are shoved into the corner, and the chairs and the babies piled out of the way, and the real celebration of the evening begins. Then Tamoszius Kuszleika, after replenishing himself with a pot of beer, returns to his platform, and, standing up, reviews the scene; he taps authoritatively upon the side of his violin, then tucks it carefully under his chin, then waves his bow in an elaborate flourish, and finally smites the sounding strings and closes his eyes, and floats away in spirit upon the wings of a dreamy waltz. His companion follows, but with his eyes open, watching where he treads, so to speak; and finally Valentinavyczia, after waiting for a little and beating with his foot to get the time, casts up his eyes to the ceiling and begins to say - "Broom! Broom! Broom!"

The company pairs off quickly, and the whole room is in motion. Apparently nobody knows how to waltz, but that is nothing of any consequence - there is music, and they dance, each as he pleases, just as before they sang. Most of them prefer the "two-step," especially the young, with whom it is in fashion. The older people have dances from home, strange and complicated steps which they execute with grave solemnity. Some do not dance anything at all, but simply hold each other's hands and allow the undisciplined joy of motion to express itself with their feet...

When Tamoszius and his companions stop for a rest, as perforce they must, now and then, the dancers halt where they are and wait patiently. They never seem to tire, and there is no place for them to sit down if they did. It is only for a minute, anyway, for the leader starts up again, in spite of all the protests of the other two. This time it is another sort of dance, a Lithuanian dance. Those who prefer to, go on with the two-step, but the majority go through an intricate series of motions, resembling more fancy skating than a dance. The climax of it is a furious prestissimo, at which the couples seize hands and begin a mad qhirling. This is quite irresistible, and everyone in the room joins in, until the place becomes a maze of flying skirts and bodies, quite dazzling to look upon...

After this there is beer for every one, the musicians included, and the revelers take a long breath and prepare for the great event of the evening, which is the acziavimas. The acziavimas is a ceremony which, once begun, will continue for three or four hours, and it involves one uninterrupted dance. The guests form a great ring, locking hands, and, when the music starts up, begin to move around in a circle. In the centre stands the bride, and one by one, the men step into the enclosure and dance with her. Each dances for several minutes - as long as he pleases; it is a very merry proceeding, with laughter and singing, and when the guest has finished, he finds himself face to face with Teta Elzbieta, who holds the hat. Into it he drops a sum of money - a dollar, or perhaps five dollars, according to his power, and his estimate of the value of the privilege. The guests are expected to pay for this entertainment; if they be proper guests, they will see that there is a neat sum left over for the bride and groom to start life upon.

Most fearful they are to contemplate, the expenses of this entertainment. They will certainly be over two hundred dollars, and may be three hundred; and three hundred dollars is more than the year's income of many a person in this room.

## ADVICE TO THE IMMIGRANT GOING OVERSEAS

## 1914

The greatest wave of Lithuanian immigrants came to these shores between 1899 and 1914. Some 250,000 Lithuanians made the trip across the Atlantic. They were semi-literate peasants for the most part in need of basic information about immigration. The editor of Tevyne, V. K. Rackauskas, prepared a manual for the would-be immigrant on the eve of the First World War. This manual or guide was based on the personal experiences of previous travelers. Therefore, it could be deemed to represent the procedures faced by immigrants between 1899 and 1914. The excerpts which follow are representative of the 290-page book.

Source: V. K. Rackauskas, Amerika arba rinkinys ivairiu faktu, zinotinu Amerikoje gyvenantiems ir cion atkeliaujantiems lietuviams, New York, Tevyne Press, 1915.

4. The Most Convenient Time To Travel.

Traveling to North America, that is, to the United States and Canada, is best accomplished in the spring. It is very hot in the cities of the United States in the summer. Our people are not acclimatized to this heat. Traveling in the winter months is not recommended, because the journey itself is uncomfortable. Another reason for not going in the winter is the fact that the factories in many American cities have a work slowdown. Many people are out of work during the winter and suffer from want. If you come in the winter you can be sure of two calamities: you will fall into adject poverty dragging your family into it as well, and secondly, you will contribute to the hardship of other unemployed immigrants. Coming in the spring is another matter. If you cannot find work in the cities, you will still be able to survive; finially, it is not difficult to find farm employment in the countryside during the summer months.

The best time to journey to South America, that is, to Brazil and Argentina, is in the summer, because that is the rainy season. During our winter months in Lithuania, South America suffers from the hot summer season.

5. Where Should One Purchase The Shipcard

Hundreds and even thousands of agents and representatives are making a living out of the fact that people are traveling from Europe to America. There are agents who send their representatives to the frontiers and try to cajole the people by all manners into migrating to America, promising them not only work, but mountains of gold as well. While hoodwinking the people, they represent only their own selfish interests and seek profit. Therefore, one must not trust these soft-talking systers. It is adviseable to go directly to the offices of the shipping companies or to a trustworthy Lithuanian agents firm. It is best to approach acquaintances or relatives in America, asking them to provide the shipcard and send it to you in Lithuania. If you do not have friends or relatives in America, it is advised to write to a well-known Lithuanian steamship ticket firm in America. A directory of such firms is provided at the end of this book. It should be failry simple to choose the best firm. We are able to indicate the following Lithuanian agencies as being the oldest in America: 1. A. Olszewskis, 3252 So. Halstead St., Chicago, Illinois; 2. J. M. Tananevice, 3249 So. Morgan St., Chicago, Illinois; 3. J. J. Paukstis and Co., 120 Grand St., Brooklyn, New York; 4. "Keleivis" Agency, 28 W. Broadway, So. Boston, Massachusetts and others. The above-mentioned agents publish their own newspapers: A. Olszewskis - "Lietuva," J. M. Tananevice - "Katalikas," J. J. Paukstis and Co. - "Vienybe Lietuvninku," etc. Thus, these agents are also civic leaders in the Lithuanian community. They are trustworthy people.

We repeat for your convenience, that one can approach the shipping companies directly. Persons traveling through the port of Libau can contact the Russian-American Steamship Company office in Libau (Kurhaus Prospekt No. 2).

6. A List of Shipping Companies.

Traveling through Germany, the best shipping lines are the following: North Deutscher Lloyd and Hamburg American Line. Traveling through Holland, the proper line is the Holland-American Line. The Red Star Line should be taken from Belgium. If you want to travel on a British ship you can purchase a steamship ticket in Libau because several British lines maintain offices there.

Below is a list of several shipping companies with information about the port of leave; furthermore we list the central offices and/or agency addresses:

1. The Russian-American Line (Vostocno-Aziatskoje Parochodnoje Obscestvo), travels between Libau and New York. Address: Kurhaus Prospekt No. 2; In New York - 27 Broadway.

2. North Deutscher Lloyd, travels between: a) Bremen and New York; b) Bremen and Philadelphia; c) Bremen and Baltimore; d) Bremen and Galveston; and e) between Hamburg and New York. American offices: 5 Broadway, New York, New York and 42-45 Broadway, New York, New York.

4. Holland-American Line, travels between Rotterdam and New York. Office - 39 Broadway, New York, New York.

5. Cunard Line, travels between Liverpool and New York. Office: 21 State Street, New York, New York.

6. American Line, sails between South Hampton and New York, Liverpool and Philadelphia. Office: 9 Broadway, New York, New York.

7. Anchor Line, travels between Glasgow and New York. Address of the office: 17 Broadway, New York, New York.

8. White Star Line, travels between Liverpool and New York, Liverpool and Boston. Office: 9 Broadway, New York, New York.

7. The Cost of Steamship Tickets

The cost of steamship tickets often changes, but the changes are not great. Therefore, one can get a fair estimate from the figures given below which should be indicative of the fare to America. We quote the third class steamship fare (steerage):

| | From Libau (in Roubles) | From Antwerpen (in Marks) |
|---|---|---|
| To New York.................. | 82 | 170 |
| To Philadelphia............. | 88 | |
| To Boston.................... | 82 | |
| To Quebec, Canada........... | 82 | 150 |
| Buenos Aires, Argentina...... | 88 | |

| From: | Rotterdam (Marks) | Bremen (Marks) | Hamburg (Marks) |
|---|---|---|---|
| To New York.................. | 160 | 160 | 150 |
| To Philadelphia............. | | 140 | |
| To Baltimore................ | | 140 | |
| To Galveston................. | | 140 | |
| To Quebec, Canada........... | | 160 | 160 |
| Buenos Aires, Argentina...... | 200 | 180 | 200 |

Second class passengers, to be sure, pay more than those traveling third class. Generally speaking, a second class shipcard costs from 115 Roubles and up.

For infants under one year the fare is 15 Roubles. Children to 12 years of age pay half fare.

## THE LITHUANIAN-AMERICANS ON THE EVE OF LITHUANIAN INDEPENDENCE: "NATIONAL SELF-DETERMINATION FOR THE HOMELAND!"

1918

The Lithuanian-Americans gave aid and assistance to their brethren in war-town Lithuania. The course of the First World War and the proclamation of President Woodrow Wilson's Fourteen Points heartened the Lithuanian-Americans. A number of political rallies were held in the larger communities in America. The largest wartime rally of politically active Lithuanian-Americans took place in New York City on March 13-14, 1918. The resolutions adopted show the development of political sophistication which led to a universal demand for national self-determination for the homeland.

The Convention of Lithuanians residing in America took place in New York City, March 13-14, 1918. Over 1,200 delegates took part in it and adopted the following resolutions:

WHEREAS,

1. Lithuania is an ethnographic, cultural, economic, and political entity;

2. The historical past of Lithuania, as well as the trend of events today, tender the Lithuanian nationality the indisputable right to restore the sovereign Lithuanian State.

3. The Lithuanian nationality is guided solely by self-determination in endeavoring to shape its political future and destiny.

4. The free development of the cultural and economic potentialities of any nationality is possible only when its land enjoys complete economic independence.

5. To decide fully its own political destiny is the birthright of every nationality.

6. The throes of this war have made the Lithuanian questions one of international significance and hence a subject for the coming international peace-conference.

7. An international congress alone - not those warring powers who are bent on enslaving Lithuania - is competent to guarantee to the people of Lithuania the freedom of its political life.

8. Woodrow Wilson, our Honorable President, is of the opinion, as expressed in his address to the United States Senate on January 22, 1918, that peace is neither desirable nor possible when it fails to recognize or accept the principle that the rights of states come from the will of the people, and that there is no law in existence that permits of trafficking in nationalities as if they were mere chattels....

After deliberating on the political condition of Lithuania, the Convention of Lithuanians in America therefore resolved that

1. The formation of an independent, democratic state within Lithuanian ethnographic boundaries, with only such deviations therefrom as are entirely indispensible for the economic life of the country, is absolutely vital to the welfare of Lithuania;

2. That the independence of Lithuania should be guaranteed by the Peace Conference, wherein Lithuanian representatives should be permitted to participate, and

3. That the resolutions of this convention be forwarded to Woodrow Wilson, our Honorable President, as representative of the United States Government, the protector and defender of the small and oppressed nationalities, and to all the other governments of the Allied and neutral nations.

As regards the form of government, the Convention of Lithuanians in America adopted the following:

WHEREAS,

1. The freedom and rights of the people can be best safeguarded in a democratic form of government;

2. The Lithuanian nationality consists chiefly of laboring people, and

3. The spirit of democracy has been ever present among Lithuanians, and

Leaving to the citizens of Lithuania themselves the right to establish a form of government and standing by the principles of democracy,

WE THEREFORE RESOLVE THAT

1. The principles of genuine democracy and the republican form of government be introduced and established in the Lithuanian State;

2. Every citizen of Lithuania, irrespective of race, faith, sex or class, shall enjoy equal political rights;

3. Freedom of speech, press, assembly, organization, religion and freedom of conscience, of person and home be recognized, and

4. Nationalization of natural resources and public service institutions be allowed only in so far as they do not trespass on the rights and freedom of the individual.

As regards the relations to Poles, the Convention adopted the following:

Cognizant of Polish intrigue and propaganda for the purpose of compelling a union of Lithuania and Poland into one body politic, or to force access through Lithuania to the Baltic Sea, the Convention, and all Lithuanians, protest most vehemently, and declare that the pretentions of Poland are utterly without foundation, contrary to the spirit of the times, and, if realized, would absolutely destroy the integrity and independence of Lithuania.

The Lithuanians shall make suitable guarantees for the freest cultural development of all peoples of whatsoever creed or race, inhabitants of Lithuania.

Conclusion.

The foregoing demonstrates clearly, we hope, that the soul of the Lithuanian nationality has always craved independence, but has not for a long time had the opportunity to speak out.

This war presented such an opportunity and immediately demands for independence proved to be voiced in unison by the entire Lithuanian race.

The independence of Lithuania is now an ideal so deeply implanted in the minds of the Lithuanian people that any solution which would seek to unite Lithuania to any other nation against her will would meet not only with the most vigorous opposition, but would most certainly cause that country to revolt with the object of attaining complete freedom. Peaceful cultural and economic development would thus be marred by conditions of bloody strife.

The resolution cited above and adopted by Lithuanians everywhere - in Lithuania, Russia, and the United States - point out that every Lithuanian political party agrees to the following:

1. That the form of government must be that of a democratic republic;

2. That the component parts of Lithuania, now unnaturally separated from one another, must be joined into a single political, economic, and cultural unit with an outlet to the sea - which means that Lithuania Minor, now under the German yoke, should be joined to Lithuania Major so that a territory situated on both sides of the river Nieman to its mouth and peopled since the remotest times by none other than Lithuanians would again be righteously united, and

3. That the sovereign rights of Lithuania be restored and guaranteed at the coming peace conference.

## OCCUPATIONS OF LITHUANIAN IMMIGRANTS

Lithuanian writers estimate that before 1899, 275,000 Lithuanian immigrants came to the United States. In 1899 a separate classification was established by the United States Government. Thus, we are able to determine with accuracy that between 1899 and 1914, an additional 252,294 Lithuanians entered the country. This mass numbering between 455,000 and 700,000 in 1930 constituted a large working force. Professor Joseph S. Roucek in his study American Lithuanians gives us a concise description of the vocational pursuits of the Lithuanian immigrants and their offspring in the United States.

....But only a minority of American Lithuanians are farmers. Most of them associate farming with the ruinous taxes and unprofitable drudgery it was their lot to experience in the home country, and they have turned to industrial pursuits instead. They are found as foundry men in Western Pennsylvania; as weavers in the cotton mills of New England and the silk mills of Paterson, New Jersey as tanners in Philadelphia, hatmakers in New York, dockworkers in Cleveland, tailors in Brooklyn, Baltimore and Chicago. Many are employed in the packing houses in Chicago, in the oil and sugar refineries around New York, and in the shoe factories in Binghamton, New York, and Brockton, Massachusetts.

In general they belong to the lower working class. The second generation, however, tends to enter the professional class.

## VULGATE LITHUANIAN:

## THE LITHUANIAN LANGUAGE IN AN AMERICAN SETTING

> The Lithuanian vocabulary is copious. Although Lithuanian is an archaic Indo-European language, it has the ability to assimilate foreign words and transmute them into Lithuanophonic terms. A Vulgate Lithuanian vocabulary or _patois_ has been developed by the Lithuanian immigrants in this country. The process began in the 1880s and has continued to this very day, witness: _hipiai_ (hippies), _besingas_ (busing), _dzetas_ (jet), and _velferininkas_ (welfare recipient).

...a close scrutiny of Lithuanian American newspapers, books, local notices and church bulletins will disclose that a peculiar speech was and is developing among immigrants. The everyday Lithuanian language has undergone some special changes in vocabulary. Thus, the English phrase: the sandwich might have spoiled, is rendered: "_Senvicius gal jau susispoilines_." Or, the boarder likes beer is expressed: "_Burdingierius laikina byra_." Algirdas Margeris has assembled a 366-page study of such loanwords, entitled _Amerikos lietuviai ir angliskuju skoliniu zodynas, 1872-1949_ (The Lithuanian Americans and A Dictionary of English Loanwords," Chicago, 1956)...

The Vulgate Lithuanian vocabulary is quite varied. Many of the words are nothing more than transliterations of English words: _anest_ (honest), _ard laif_ (hard life), _fani_ (funny) (_viz._, jis ne tik fani, bet ir kreizi or He is not only funny, but crazy as well), _flet_ (flat), etc. But many loanwords are somewhat Lithuanized: _aibolis_ (highball), _alperis_, _elperis_ (helper), _baketas_ (bucket), _begidzius_ (baggage), _cencius_ (chance), _dypas_ (depot), _dzela_ (jail), _fornisas_ (furnace), _garbicius_ (garbage), _grainderis_ (grinder), _poizinas_ (poison), _singelis_ (a single person), _strytas_ (street), _trokas_ (truck), _karas_ (car), _vacyti_ (to watch), _vuordas_ (ward), and others.

A study of such terms will disclose certain linguistic tendencies. Thus, the many English nouns with the ending "y" will receive an "e" in Lithuanian: baby will become _beibe_, battery will become _betre_, _blaine_ is blind; ball becomes _bole_; brandy is _brande_ or _brende_, dolly is _dole_, daisy is _deize_. Other English words ending in "y" also become transformed foundry (_fandre_), candy (_kende_), laundry (_lendre_), even "pay" (_pede_). Certain English words ending in a consonant also take an "e": dish (_dise_), dress (_drese_), gang (_genge_), rails (_reles_), ham (_ame_).

Some English nouns ending in vowels, take a Lithuanian "-sas" instead of the customary "-as" in the nominative case. Thus: _boisas_ (boy), _drinksas_ (drink), _liumpsas_ (lump), _tinksas_ (thing), _triksas_ (trick), etc.

Certain English words are transformed in a peculiar manner. For example, the words bekerne (bakery), bucerne (butchershop), pikcerne (photo studio), groserne (grocery) are formed by taking an English phonetic root and adding the Slavic (Polish) suffix -erne. On the other hand, bresine (brass factory) is formed with the Lithuanian suffix ine. There are other words with Slavic suffixes: biznierius (businessman), tycerka (lady teacher), politikierius (politician).

At least a thousand English words have become international and have found their way into Lithuanian, just as they have done so into other languages. Thus, it is proper to use auditorija, banditas, doleris, filmas, langunas, lincas, lyderis, piknikas, pudingas, snobas, kaubojus (auditorium, bandit, dollar, film, lagoon, lynch. leader, picnic, pudding, snob, cowboy) in literary Lithuanian.

There are instances of purely Lithuanian terms being coined on the basis of American English concepts: naryste (membership), vajus (drive, as membership drive narystes vajus), antvalandziai or virsvalandziai (overtime).

Generally speaking, the Lithuanian immigrants, of peasant stock for the most part, without proper schooling or rudiments in the niceties of their own native tongue, quickly succumbed to the influences of American English. They eventually became more and more careless in distinguishing between the grammar and vocabularies of the two languages. Furthermore, they were exposed to concepts not encountered in the homeland. They were unable to find or remember Lithuanian equivalents for these terms. Thus, they absorbed many special English terms picked up in the factory, at school, in the army and at work. They mingled English with their native Lithuanian dialects. It was no longer necessary to communicate in a literate Lithuanian language which served no useful function in the new world. There is a large everyday Vulgate vocabulary which has replaced Lithuanian equivalents, to wit: byras (beer - alus), barne (barn - darzine), cizelis (chysel - kaltas), beikeris (baker - kepejas), beibe (baby - kudikis), eme (ham - kumpis), bliuberes (blueberries - melynes), auzas (house - namas), ameris (hammer - plaktukas), bymas (beam - rastas), bencius (bench - suolas), bridzas (bridge - tiltas), (daiperiai (diapers - vystyklai), etc. There are also man specifically American terms: aisbaksis (icebox - ledaune), bildingas (building - pastatas), bomas (bum - dykaduonis, valkata), drajeris (drier - dziovintuvas), dzenitorius (janitor - namsargis), fenas (fan - vesintuvas, veduokle), grynauze (greenhouse - siltadarzis), drugstoris (drugstore - vaistine), kempe (camp - stovykla), kortas (court - teismas). Finally there is an "American Lithuanian mode" which follows no norm and which haphardly borrows from one or the other language. For example, all Lithuanians are familiar with the word purvas (mud) which was changed into dortas (dirt). Later an adjectival form based on the Lithuanian purvinas (muddy) or English dirty was coined, to wit: dortinas. Those who prefer to use English, when speaking Lithuanian do not follow rules of gender and simply say" "Mano rankos visai dorti" (My hands are completely dirty)....

THE UNITED STATES SECRETARY OF STATE, HUGHES,

TO THE UNITED STATES COMMISSIONER IN RIGA, YOUNG

Source: U.S. Department of State, Foreign Relations of the United States, Papers Relating to...1922, Vol. II, Washington, G.P.O., 1938, pp. 973-74.

860. n.01/52a: Telegram
The Secretary of State to the
Commissioner at Riga (Young)

Washington, July 25, 1922, 4 p.m.

Advise Foreign Offices of Estonia, Latvia and Lithuania as nearly at the same time as possible on the morning of July 28, that the United States extend to each full recognition. The fact will be communicated to the Press at Washington for publication in the morning papers of July 28, and the following statement will be made:

The Governments of Estonia, Latvia and Lithuania have been recognized either de jure or de facto by the principal Governments of Europe and have entered into treaty relations with their neighbors.

In extending to them recognition on its part, the Government of the United States takes cognizance of the actual existence of these Governments during a considerable period of time and of the successful maintenance within their borders of political and economical stability.

The United States has consistently maintained that the disturbed conditions of Russian affairs may not be made the occasion for alienation of Russian territory, and this principle is not deemed to be impinged by the recognition at this time of the Governments of Estonia, Latvia and Lithuania which have been set up and maintained by indigenous population.

Pending legislation by Congress to establish regular diplomatic representation Mr. Young will continue as Commissioner of the United States and will have the rank of Minister. Request from respective Governments temporary recognition pending formal application for exequatures of John P. Hurley, Charles H. Albrecht, and Clement S. Edwards, consuls at Riga, Reval and Kovno, respectively.

Signed: Hughes.

## OUTSTANDING LITHUANIAN AMERICANS

## 1938

The Lithuanian-Americans were not far behind other nationality groups in seeking education and economic betterment. By the late 1930s the Lithuanian-American community could point with pride to a number of leaders in the arts, education, business, and sports. The sociologist Joseph S. Roucek provides us with a catalogue of accomplished Lithuanian-Americans.

Source: Joseph Roucek, American Lithuanians, New York, 1939.

American-Lithuanian Musicians, Actors, Artists.

Mikas Petrauskas, composer of a very large number of popular Lithuanian songs, about 20 Lithuanian operettas and a Lithuanian opera, was the first musically trained Lithuanian to work among his people in America...Petrauskas was born on September 29, 1873 and died in Lithuania on March 3, 1937. He first came to the United States on June 13, 1907, but after a concert tour of Lithuanian settlements, returned to Italy for further studies. He came back to America again in 1909....In addition to writing music, he did much to popularize Lithuanian folk dances, and was an able organizer of Lithuanian singing choirs. He maintained at different times three conservatories of music, in Brooklyn, in Chicago, and in Boston. With the exception of his opera, "Egle-Zalciu Karaliene," presented in Boston in 1924, his compositions were of a light, popular character, utilizing extensively motives from the numerous Lithuanian folksongs. His exceptionally pleasant personality, unlimited energy, and remarkable teaching talents, together with his musical works have endeared him to American Lithuanians. He is universally considered to be the most popular Lithuanian composer and the foremost worker in the field of Lithuanian folk song.

There are other well-known musical leaders, Anna Kaska, contralto, was one of the first singers to be chosen for stardom with the Metropolitan Opera Company from radio auditions; she was born of Lithuanian parents in Hartford, Connecticut, and after studying two years at the Hartford Conservatory of Music went to Lithuania and later to Italy for further study. Joseph Babravicius has returned from New York to his native land and joined the National Opera there. Emilija Mickunas of Philadelphia and Misses Marijona Rakauskaite and Margareta Cesnaviciute are well known as singers. Professor Joseph Zilevicius, former director of the Conservatory of Music at Klaipeda, and composer, now lives in America. Among other prominent Lithuanian musicians in the United States are Alexander Aleksis, formerly of the Conservatory of Warsaw; the violinist, Professor

J. Zidanavicius; Anthony Pocius, Director of the Beethoven Conservatory of Music of Chicago; Peter Sarpalius, composer; John Cizauskas and his brother, Reverend Joseph Cizauskas. Helen Mickunas and F. Jakavicius are connected with the Chicago Civic Opera, Ralph Juska with the Philadelphia Civic Opera and S. Paskewicz with the Hippodrome Opera Company.

In the field of acting, Ivan Lebedoff is a featured player in Hollywood, where Shirley White also plays in motion pictures. June Barron, Betty Dumbris and Helen Brown were members of the Ziegfield Follies, while M. Taparauskas is a member of the Globe Theatre.

The late V. D. Brenner-Baranauskas was the designer of the American Lincoln cent. Louis Rosenthal is a well-known sculptor. M. J. Sileikis is connected with the Chicago Art Institute. In the field of painting, Ignas Ylekis of Chicago stands out and Jonas Szileika was awarded a first prize by the Chicago Art Institute while he lived in America.

American Lithuanian Men of Letters.

The American Lithuanian group is very rich in talented literary men: K. Jurgelionis and J. Jokubaitis, poets; S. E. Vitaitis, editor of the daily "Vienybe"; J. Tysliava, poet and editor of the monthly "Lietuva"; Rev. Casimir Urbonavicius (Jonas Kmitas), poet and editor-in-chief of "Darbininkas"; Rev. Joseph Zidanavicius (Seiriju Juozas), writer and dramatist; Rev. Anthony Milukas, editor, publisher, writer; Nagurauskas of Baltimore, author of several successful dramas; Leonard Simutis (Silelis), editor-in-chief of "Draugas," publicist, writer and poet; Rev. J. Navickas, publicist, writer, historian; K. S. Karpius, editor of "Dirva", publicist and writer of many novels; Rev. John Balkunas, editor of "Amerika" and publicist. Among other prominent literary men are Rev. Francis Vaitukaitis, St. Jasiulonis, P. Bayoras, Ant. Tulis, Jonas Sliburis, and R. Mizara. Dr. M. J. Vinikas, Secretary of the Lithuanian Alliance of America, is the author of "Economic Relations Of Lithuania" and "Diplomatic Relations of Lithuania" (thesis, American University, Washington, D.C., 1933, 1934).

In the field of education we hear of Rev. Joseph Vaitkevicius, formerly Professor of the Seminaries of Vloclavek and Vilna and the University of Lithuania, at present Professor of Theology at Marian Hills Seminary, Hinsdale, Illinois; Dr. J. Navickas, Rector of the Marianopolis College, Thompson, Connecticut; Rev. Michael Civulskis, Director of the La Salette College, Hartford, Connecticut. Dr. J. Raymond-Rimavicius lectures on Lithuanian at Columbia University; E. Ziurys is connected with Yale University; Lieut. P. Moncius, a graduate of Annapolis Academy, is now with Harvard University.

American Lithuanians in Public Office

In civic and political affairs, Casimir Kriauciunas (Kay) was Judge of the Superior Court of Seattle, Washington. William Laukaitis occupies a judicial bench in Baltimore. J. Zuris is a Chicago judge and Frank Mast, formerly Counselor of the Lithuanian Legation was Assistant District Attorney of Chicago. Dr. A. Velybus and A. Janusaitis (Janushat) are members of the Pennsylvania, and J. De

Righter-Deraitis of the Ohio State legislature. Bolic A. Degasis is Police Court Judge at Nashua, New Hampshire; W. J. Wimbiscus, Judge of the Cook County Circuit Court of Chicago, and J. P. Uvick, Judge of the City of Grosse Point, Michigan. J. Kairis, Mayor of Seatonville, Illinois, Anna C. Lakawitz, Mayor of Linndale, Ohio, and J. Vansavage, Mayor of New Philadelphia, Pennsylvania are others who have achieved prominence in civic affairs.

American Lithuanian Athletes

In the field of athletics, Jack Sharkey (Juozas Zukauskas), the former World's heavyweight champion; Billie Burke (Vincas Burkauskas), golfer; Jack Goodman, golf champion; Albina Osipavitch, member of the United States Olympic swimming team; John Macionis, member of the Yale University swimming team and record holder; Emma Shemaitis, swimming star; George Chip, former boxing champion; Yustin Sirutis, former national amateur boxing champion; Joe Bartulis, member of the White Sox baseball team; V. Tamulis, member of the New York Yankees and Newark Bears baseball teams; J. Broaca, member of the New York Yankees baseball team; B. Boken, member of the Washington Senators baseball team; Willie Scrill, an outstanding basketball professional; J. Grebauskas, captain of Princeton's basketball team; F. Lubin, captain of the United States Olympic basketball team are a few of the outstanding American Lithuanian athletes. In the field of wrestling, Carl Pojello is holder of British and European championships; Andy Kandrat and Joe Komar are strong men of the old school; Dr. Sarpolis and Jack Ganson have also made their reputation in this field.

Many American Lithuanians are active on college and university football teams. In the fall of 1935, the majority of players on the football team of the Catholic University were Lithuanians. Others who are famous are Ed. Krause, Plansky, Adomavicius, Dranginis, Miciuta, Jablonsky and Karpovich.

## LITHUANIANS AT THE NEW YORK WORLD'S FAIR

## 1939

The Lithuanian-Americans organized a highly successful cultural program for "Lithuanian Day" at the New York World's Fair on September 10, 1939. Joseph B. Laucka, Chairman of the World's Fair Lithuanian Day Committee, expressed the feeling of pride in the accomplishments of Lithuanians on both sides of the Atlantic.

Source: Text of speech in Lithuanian Day New York World's Fair, September 10, 1939, New York, 1939, pp. 6-7.

When the Lithuanian Government accepted the invitation of the President of the United States to participate in the New York World's Fair, none rejoiced in that as much as the American Lithuanians. Their joy was not unfounded. The older generation of Lithuanians, which had emigrated from Lithuania when she was under suppression, put gigantic efforts before and during the World War in helping their native land to see a new dawn of free life. This undertaking was possible for them because the American people understood deeply th Lithuanian aims and efforts. The Lithuanians in this country tried to be good citizens at all times and by this they achieved a reputable name and standing for themselves and the Lithuanian nation. They believed that Lithuania should become free and independent again. They sent Lithuanian literature from the land of freedom to suppressed Lithuania where people had been forbidden to use even Lithuanian prayer books. They encouraged their fathers and brothers to fight increasingly for the freedom of their country. They sent their material support. They strove that their newly adopted country, the United States of America, should be one of the first to recognize the independence of reborn Lithuania rising from the bloody fields of battle. The dreams and the hopes of the American Lithuanians became a reality when Lithuania declared her independence on February 16, 1918, in Vilna, the historical capital of Lithuania. When she began to progress step by step, the American Lithuanians waited with feverish impatience for the opportune moment when the people of the United States would be able to see for themselves what a small nation, one of the oldest in the world and suppressed for centuries, was able to accomplish in just a few years of freedom. This long awaited moment has arrived with the Lithuanian participation in the New York World's Fair. Here Lithuania has put her efforts to show as much as possible her achievements in education, industry, commerce, agriculture and social life during the twenty years of her independence.

The tragic deprival of Klaipeda (Memel) and the major uncertainties and dangerous international complications combined to create insurmountable obstacles, which handicapped the Lithuanian Pavilion to portray its country's capabilities and status adequately. American Lithuanians, however, are quite satisfied with the results achieved by the Lithuanian Pavilion.

Here they see the Lithuanian creative power exemplified and view its progress; and even in its very simplicity they sense the presence of a heroic spirit and a deep love of a living heart.

Lithuania, participating in the New York World's Fair accepted the invitation to celebrate the national day the purposes of which are....to commemorate the 500 anniversary of King Vytautas the King.. To fulfill the program for this special day Lithuania has invited American Lithuanians to do their part. For this cooperative undertaking the World's Fair Lithuanian Day Committee was formed from the national cultural, fraternal and professional organizations which have always professed loyalty to the United States, the Lithuanian nation, and Lithuania. The Committee received close advice and suggestive leadership from the Honorable Jonas Budrys, Consul General of Lithuania. Moreover, the Lithuanian press has shown courtesy and has given generous support to the work of the Committee. And today we are glad to witness the results of the cooperative efforts of the American Lithuanians and the committee. On behalf of the Committee I wish to express my sincere gratitude to all who helped to make this Lithuanian Day a success. Today, American Lithuanians commemorating Lithuanian National Day at the Fair send their most hearty and cordial greetings to Lithuania, her leaders, statesmen and her populace and sincerely wish them a bright future, peaceful living conditions, and perpetual cultural progress.

## STATEMENT BY SUMNER WELLES,

## ACTING U.S. SECRETARY OF STATE TO THE AMERICAN PRESS

## THE BALTIC REPUBLICS

## 1940

Shortly after the Soviet forced occupation of the three Baltic Republics, the Acting Secretary of State Sumner Welles issued a public statement on the United States position regarding this aggression. This statement forms the basis of the American Pinciple of Nonrecognition of the Soviet Occupation and Incorporation fo the Baltic States into the USSR.

Source: Department of State Bulletin (Washington), Vol. III, No. 57, 1940:48.

Statement Released to the Press July 23, 1940.

During these past few days the devious proceses whereunder the political independence and territorial integrity of the three small Baltic republics - Estonia, Latvia, and Lithuania - were to be deliberately annihilated by one of their more powerful neighbors, have been rapidly drawing to their conclusion.

From the day when the peoples of these republics first gained their independent and democratic form of government, the people of the United States have watched their admirable progress in self-government with deep and sympathetic interest.

The policy of this Government is universally known. The people of the United States are opposed to predatory activities no matter whether they are carried on by the use of force or by the threat of force. They are likewise opposed to any form of intervention on the part of one state, however powerful, in the domestic concerns of any other sovereign state, however weak.

These principles constitute the very foundations upon which the existing relationship between the 21 sovereign republics of the New World rests.

The United States will continue to stand by these principles, because of the conviction of the American people that unless the doctrine in which these principles are inherent once again governs the relations between nations, the rule of reason, of justice, and of law - in other words, the basis of modern civilization itself - cannot be preserved.

## MEMORANDUMS AND STATEMENTS:

## THE LITHUANIAN AMERICAN COUNCIL'S DELEGATION

## MEETS WITH PRESIDENT FRANKLIN D. ROOSEVELT

## 1940

President Franklin Delano Roosevelt on October 15, 1940 received a delegation of the Lithuanian American Council in the White House. The spokesman for the delegation, Dr. Pius Grigaitis, read the special memorandum regarding the concern of the Lithuanian Americans over the occupation of Lithuania by the Soviet Union. An extract from the Memorandum follows.

Source: Leonardas Simutis, Lithuanian American Council, 1940-1970, Chicago, Draugas Press, 1971, pp. 458; also cf. Im Ausland-Abroad, (Augsburg). No. 10-1, April, 1948:1.

The delegation before you, Mr. President, represents most of the Lithuanian people of the United States; it is here to encourage you in the task of bringing reason and law to reign again in a distracted world.

With the world aflame, with ruthless might attempting to conquer the earth, the Lithuanian people in America were moved to great depths of sorrow when their native land and land of their forebears lost her freedom.

When Lithuanian fell, it seemed that the nations of the earth, particularly those who had recognized her as independent, were disinterested, none condemned that act of extirpation which to the Lithuanians of America seemed so needful of condemnation.

Then, on the twenty-third day of July 1940, your State Department, Mr. President, announced the attitude of the Government of the United States regarding the loss of Lithuania's independence. Among other declarations, it said:....

That was a clear, understandable and unequivocal statement of policy. It was an act of condemnation of a wrong committed by a great power against a weak nation. At last the clamor of destruction was overcome by the call to reason and justice, and our people were glad that voice came from the greatest liberty-loving nation on earth - the United States of America.

We are proud that our United States of America stands firmly behind a policy that knows no compromise with aggression.

Your courageous stand, Mr. President, on the side of justice, law and reason enkindled the flame of hope - a hope that Lithuania may again take her place amongst the nations of the earth.

Please accept, Mr. President, the sincerest gratitude, esteem and also the profound admiration of the Lithuanians of America for that declaration.

> After listening to the delegation's remarks and upon acceptance of the memorandum, President Roosevelt outdid the Lithuanians in his reply. He went on to say that the United States would do everything in its power to hasten the day of independence, and that after the war Lithuanian and the other enslaved nations would be free.

It pleased me to see that you, American citizens of Lithuanian origin, are so deeply concerned with the fate of your mother country. My ancestors came to this country long before you came. They were from Holland. Regardless of the fact that many years have passed, I still consider Holland as the land of my forefathers; the misfortunes that befell Holland pains me deeply and I shall do everything in my power to make Holland a free country again. The ancestors of my wife came from Belgium, naturally, the fate of Belgium is in no less a degree a concern of mine. Therefore, I understand perfectly your feelings concerning the fate of Lithuania.

But let me tell you that you have made here two mistakes; the first mistake is in your address that you gave me. It is stated here that Lithuania has lost her independence. It is a mistake to say so. Lithuania did not lose her independence. Lithuania's independence was only temporarily put aside. Time will come and Lithuania will be free again. This will happen much sooner than you may expect. The other mistake as I observed was made by one of your speakers when he referred to Lithuania as a very small state. Look at the Latin American Republics and you will see that there are even smaller states than Lithuania, but they live a free and happy life. It is not fit even to talk about the smallness of Lithuania for even the smallest nation has the same right to enjoy independence as the largest nation.

## LITHUANIAN CULTURE IN TWENTIETH CENTURY AMERICA

1949

Monsignor K. Urbonavicius - Jonas Kmitas - the famed Lithuanian-American journalist and novelist, draws an outline of the development of Lithuanian culture in America. He was an advocate of the preservation of the Lithuanian language as a cultural vehicle. His views form the ideological basis of the Lithuanian Roman Catholic activist and intellectual in America. Jonas Kmitas admits that the loss of independence of the homeland has shut off the natural cultural source, yet he is very optimistic about the cultural potential of the displaced persons arriving in America.

Source: Lithuanian Franciscan Press, 1950 Sventieji Metai, Brooklyn, 1950.

"I was born in Lithuania, lived with my folks,
I set out to wander, to search for fortune."

Thus sang our people going to Prussia, from thence they took ship to America. The trip across the ocean was not always calm. Storms would arise.

"A billow comes aroaring, it sets our ship arolling,--
There is no fear greater, no death more fearsome."

And finally the traveler reaches America, that dreamed of land of freedom and gold. How will one live here? Of course, cheerfully and with luck. But will one not suffer from disappointment? The newcomers gave no thought to this last question. Their eyes were affixed to the gigantic buildings of New York stretching even to the clouds. Will it be the same everywhere? One does not even think about that. The cities, in truth, are great, but not always clean. But there are riches here! Alas, not for us. The immigrant begins to pine for the moss-covered cottage, for the meadows and fields of Lithuania, for the Nemunas, the Neris, the Sesupe... Most of all one longs for the mother tongue. And so the immigrant begins to value Lithuania, as one who has lost his very health...

In one way or another, one settles down in America. One takes work. Oh, how it is difficult to find suitable work in this land! The immigrant begins to concern himself with creating a Lithuanian environment, wherein the native language would resound. This is a necessity, for having left the fatherland, one must create a substitute elsewhere. And the immigrants began to band together in mutual aid societies, named after saints for the most part. This was just the beginning. Later the larger colonies will organize parishes, build churches in order to hear the word of God in the native language and sing sacred hymns in Lithuanian. Much drudgery, labor and finances are placed in the building of churches, but the immigrants reach their goal: the spires of Lithuanian churches reach to heaven in many colonies, bells and organs play, and the crowds kneel and sing "Pulkim ant keliu"....Everything is like in Lithuania....

Not only mutual aid societies arose, but social organizations with wide purpose, whose conventions or seimai were akin to great national festivals: everywhere one would hear the Lithuanian language and song. Lithuanian stores appeared, wherein the consumers could freely converse in Lithuanian. The Lithuanian housewives were thrilled that they did not have to go to English stores and twist their tongues or show by pointing what it was they wanted. And so the Lithuanian American life was gradually ordered. A continuous flow of Lithuanian immigrants came from the homeland. These immigrants were handsome, green, lively youths. There was no end to weddings. The newly-weds formed Lithuanian families, and their children spoke Lithuanian at home.

No small number of intellectuals - priests and laymen - came over. They began to spread the Lithuanian word and book: newspapers were published, books printed, community organizations formed, Lithuanian libraries set up. Monasteries and convents were founded for Lithuanian religious orders. Schools were constructed. National halls, old peoples homes and orphanages were founded. European calibre priests, like Mikukas, Staniukynas, Kaupas, Kaulakis, Sedvydis, Kemesis, Dargis and others became the resourceful and intelligent leaders of the immigrants. Somewhat later the Marian Order was revived. The Marians had a number of well-trained spiritual leaders: Bucys, Vaitkevicius, Kudirka, Kulikauskas, Navickas. They were writers, editors, youth leaders, rectors of seminaries and colleges. It would appear that Providence had sent these inspired leaders to direct the religious and national cultural work of the immigrants. It was a Golden Age of the Immigration. This period lasted up to the First World War...

During the war immigration from Lithuania ceased. But the immigration had a surplus of Lithuanianism to see it through these dark years. However the enthusiasm subsided because of the great hardship that Lithuania had to undergo during the war years. It appears that the beloved fatherland, becoming a battleground, would be totally destroyed. When it became apparent that both Germany and Russia would collapse, the Lithuanians began to fight for their freedom and independence. The Lithuanian Americans supported their brothers' efforts. Huge donations were made to aid Lithuania. It was not a rare occurence when a large colony would raise 20-30,000 dollars to assist Lithuania.

After Lithuania had won her independence, her relations with the immigration became very close and cordial. The Lithuanian-American youth inspired by the bravery of the Lithuanian Army, suddenly felt an inspiration of Lithuanian patriotism. When at times a motion picture film of marching Lithuanian Army units, not only would the old-timers, but the young people as well would break out in applause. Young girls would thrill at the handsome features of the soldiers and their smart marching stride. "We never thought that there would be such handsome and rugged men over there," they would comment. The Americans like victors in war, sports and life in general. Learning that small and worn-out Lithuania was able to fend off three powerful aggressors and not only defend itself, but create a new viable state as well made an impression on the young Lithuanian-Americans who felt a surge of pride in their heroic kinsmen. The athletes of the immigrations especially wanted to get acquainted with Lithuania. Sports groups were formed which wanted to visit Lithuania. There they fraternized with Lithuania's youth and felt a kinship. Much pleasure was derived for both sides from this fraternization. There was a spiritual rebirth of Lithuanianism among the young Lithuanian Americans.

This was especially apparent in Marianapolis College. Under Rev. Dr. J. Navickas Lithuanianism was fostered in the College. Of course, the language of instruction was English. Yet the Lithuanian language courses were pursued very seriously. There were many language courses and they were a required subject (at the time the College did not have non-Lithuanian students). The professors demanded much, and the students were forced to cram Lithuanian grammar and practice the correct pronunciation of words. This was the hardest. One brought up in English found it difficult to capture the soft Lithuanian sounds and diphthongs. Come what may, the students had to learn to pronounce Lithuanian words properly. During the recreation period the rector saw to it that the spoke only in Lithuanian. Those who did not observe the rules brought down the wrath of the rector upon themselves. The results of this "Lithuanian" training were startling: some students who had enrolled in college knowing only a few Lithuanian words, after four years became well versed in Lithuanian grammar, syntax and phonetics as well. There were students whose papers and recitals in Lithuanian were a pleasure to observe.

Marianapolis College - or to be more precise - her rector Rev. Dr. Navickas - established the Student and Professional Association, whose organ "Studentu Zodis" was edited there. The student acts and conventions were veritable Lithuanian festivities. Many guests would attend to socialize in a Lithuanian atmosphere.

Alas, on September 2, 1941 the beloved college rector and Marian Provincial Father, Dr. Navickas suddenly died. Much, much Lithuanianism went to the grave with him. Three months later the ghastly attack on Pearl Harbor brought the United States into the Second World War. Dark, sad days came. Lithuania was occupied and made a martyr by the totalitarian powers. And - what is most tragic - is the fact that the allies in whose ranks many Lithuanian youths gave their lives - as is borne out later - not for Lithuania's liberation, but for her further incarceration....

And among the young people Lithuanianism began to decline rapidly. It is difficult to analyze the psyche of the American-born Lithuanian. While they were charmed by Lithuania's independence, everything appeared fine, pleasant and hopeful. But when this lantern was extinguished, it became difficult to fathom their hearts. Perhaps a disappointment and scepticism forced its way in. It suffices that they no longer concerned themselves with Lithuanianism and the fate of Lithuania. Possibly it is a mistaken speculation, but it appears that their re-Lithuanianization (atlietuvinimas) has become a difficult and almost impossible task.

In all truthfulness, even before the war there were unpleasant manifestations as far as Lithuanianism is concerned. During the Knights of Lithuania Convention in Boston (which convened in 1935 or 1936) one delegate offered that the Knights of Lithuania conventions and meetings in general use only the English language. The convention chairman, who was also the president of the organization at the time, Mr. Lapinskas declared that this suggestion will be rejected without the slightest doubt. But the discussion by the delegates is interesting. The question was debated. One young delegate arose to speak. He had come to this country from Lithuania only a few years before. Here he completed high school and was well educated in the English language. He demonstrated in perfect English that the Knights of Lithuania meetings should only use English because everyone knows English and that the majority do not use Lithuanian or do not even understand the language. Howbeit, the argument appeared logical. The convention delegates greeted the speaker with applause. It seemed that Mr. Lapinskas was mistaken.

However a delegate from New Jersey asked for the floor and his talk surprised everyone. First of all, he apologized that he will speak in English, because he is only able to converse with his parents in Lithuanian. And this youth, born in America, hardly conversant in Lithuanian, began to defend the rights of the Lithuanian language! He declared that it is natural for the Knights of Lithuania to speak Lithuanian. This is why they are called the Knights of Lithuania. Thus, it would be contradictory to introduce the English language as the only medium and it would run counter to common sense and the K. of L. Constitution! Of course, the English language will not be denied; those who do not speak Lithuanian must needs converse in English, but the meetings of the Knights of Lithuania must be Lithuanian language lessons and exercises so that those who are not proficient in the language may learn.

The thunderous applause that followed clearly showed that the convention delegates were more in favor of the arguments of the second speaker than those of the former. Lapinskas had guessed correctly: the convention rejected the English language proposal. However, the talk of the New Jersey delegate was not recorded in the minutes. Everything remained as before. The Knights of Lithuania continued to use both languages. And the columns of Vytis remained bilingual and spotty, the Lithuanian language continued to give way to English. This incident of the Knights of Lithuanian convention shows that there is a Lithuanian patriotism in the hearts of the American-born youth. However, there is nothing and no one to inspire them.

Lithuanians who do not speak English do not bring any benefit to their ancestral homeland. There is no use of people who hide their nationality by changing their surnames. It is said that they feel and will always feel that they are Lithuanians. Perhaps, because it is not easy to get rid of one's parents' cultural heritage. But even if they entertain such feelings they will not tell anyone about them. Otherwise, why did they change their surnames....

Yet by one way or another one must strive to save them. Not everyone has irrevocably rejected his heritage. Maybe the Lithuanian displaced persons coming to this country will be able to perform their national mission by inspiring the indifferent Lithuanian-Americans?....

....Several editors from the displaced persons camps who have arrived to this country have begun to work for Vytis, Amerika, Lietuviu Zinios, Varpelis, Kalifornijos Lietuvis. This is a plus for Lithuanian culture. A number of European intellectuals have come to the assistance of Draugas, Darbininkas, Zvaigzde, Laivas, Garsas - they are infusing a healthy, creative and inspirational Lithuanianism in the Lithuanian-American press. It is a pleasure to point out their assistance.... Finally, there are the countless works of prose and poetry of the exiles which will serve to revive a love of Lithuania and which will introduce a pure, literate and stylistic Lithuanian language. The new-comers will serve a national mission when they will integrate our society. And even those newcomers, who do not undertake literary or civic activities, will by their use of the standard literary Lithuanian language will re-Lithuanianize a great many immigrant families. And what can be said about the future leaders of the Catholic Ateitis and Pavasaris Federations - and the other leaders and activists of Lithuania who did not break under the Bolshevik and Nazi yokes. Those who have suffered persecution and torture will not sit here with their hands folded!

These legions of Lithuanian civic workers will guarantee a brighter future for our immigration and for our fatherland Lithuania.

## THE LITHUANIAN CHARTER

## 1949

The Supreme Committee for Liberation of Lithuania drafted a unique document, the Lithuanian Charter (Lietuviu Charta) which formulated the ideological basis for a Lithuanian World Community. The quintessence of Lithuanianism is expressed by this basically simple code which was adopted by organized Lithuanian cultural communities throughout the free world.

### The Lithuanian Charter

Lithuanians we are born,
Lithuanians we must remain!

The Lithuanian Nation,
having hardened itself in the age-long struggle for the right to lead a free and independent existence in the lands of its forefathers, with a united will seeks to preserve, create and foster its existence, language, national and state traditions,
in order to collaborate in the universal family of man by contributine its unique national culture to progress as a fulfillment of the Almighty's Will and the vocation of free mankind.

In the name of the eternal aspirations of the Lithuanian Nation, let this LITHUANIAN CHARTER BE PROMULGATED.

1.

The Nation is a natural community of people.

No one can be forced to sever his ties with the national community.

Lithuanians scattered throughout the world constitute a single Lithuanian World Community (Pasaulio Lietuviu Bendruomene).

2.

Man has the natural right to confess (profess) and foster his nationality.

A Lithuanian remains a Lithuanian everywhere and always.

In order to preserve the existence of his ancestors' Lithuanian Nation, a Lithuanian passes on the culture to future generations to insure the eternal nature of his nationality.

3.

Language is the strongest tie of the national community. The Lithuanian language is the national honor of all Lithuanians.

4.

The life of the nation is the family.
A Lithuanian forms a Lithuanian family.

5.

The national culture is the road to international recognition and cooperation.

6.

The state is the highest organization of the national community.

National independence is the necessary condition for the development and preservation of national culture.

In order to defend and preserve the independent Lithuanian state, each Lithuanian strives by his work, knowledge, fortune and sacrifice.

7.

The school is the hearth of the national spirit.

It is the lofty duty of each Lithuanian to be a supporter of Lithuanian schools.

8.

A society is the active handmaid of national culture. A Lithuanian establishes and maintains religious, cultural, youth, self-aid, professional and other Lithuanian societies.

9.

The struggles and sacrifices of our fathers for the Lithuanian book is a testimentary obligation for all of the generations of the Lithuanian Nation.

The Lithuanian organizes and supports the printed Lithuanian word.

10.

The history of the nation is the best national school.

The Lithuanian values his national past and national customs.

The Lithuanian endeavors to be worthy of his ancestors to be able to bequeath his descendents pride and honor.

11.

National solidarity is the highest virtue of the nation. A Lithuanian fosters national solidarity.

All Lithuanians are the equal children of the nation, and among themselves they are brothers.

Each Lithuanian pays his due to national solidarity by these signs: national consciousness and Lithuanian unity.

12.

The Lithuanian national colors are: yellow-green-and-red.

The Lithuanian National Holiday is February the Sixteenth.

The Lithuanian Slogan is: "Lithuanians we are born, Lithuanians we must remain!" (Lietuviais esame me gime, lietuviais turime ir but!)

13.

The Lithuanian is loyal to the country of his residence.

The Lithuanian's relations with his non-Lithuanian neighbor are based on love and the respect for each person's freedom, honor, life, health and property.

THE SUPREME COMMITTEE
FOR LIBERATION OF
LITHUANIA

In exile, June 14, 1949.

## THE IMMIGRANT AND LITHUANIA:

## "YOU WILL BE A BETTER AMERICAN"

## 1951

The question of loyalties is a perennial one for immigrants. It was a reoccuring theme among the Lithuanian Americans. The American-born Lithuanian, for that matter, still has to resolve the problem for himself. The first to seek a compromise between "Americanism" and "Lithuanianism" was Vytautas Sirvydas, who in the 1930s coined the succinct mott: "Americans first, but Lithuanians always!" The American-born Marian Father, Frank Yancius, in an editorial in the English-language magazine, The Marian, gives a rebuttal to the Lithuanian-Americans who reject the heritage of their fathers.

Source: Editorial, The Marian, March, 1951.

In your last letter you scolded me for my so-called "Un-American" leanings and found it difficult to understand how I, who was born and raised in this glorious land of ours, can call myself a Lithuanian and concern myself so much about things that are Lithuanian. In your opinion it's downright unpatriotic for me, an American, to act so.

Well, friend, as a fellow American and Lithuanian, you are entitled to an answer. There are many reasons why I am proud of my Lithuanian heritage.

First and foremost is the simple reason that God made me a Lithuanian. He allowed me to be born and to live in America as the son of wonderful Lithuanian immigrant parents. In other words, Friend, God made me at one and the same time a Lithuanian and an American. To deny my Lithuanian ancestry would be to find fault with the handiwork of my Creator.

Next comes the God-given command to love and honor one's parents. By being ashamed of my Lithuanian origin, I would be lacking in the proper filial respect for my parents. Furthermore, all religious motives aside, I would discredit myself in the eyes of my friends and relatives, for Lithuanian blood flows in my veins.

Our America is a melting pot of cultures, a mixture of many peoples and races who have all contributed their bit to our American way of life.

To me my parents represent America. Their sweat and blood and tears, their calloused hands and aching bones, like those of countless other immigrants, have helped build this glorious land of ours into a mighty bulwark of democracy and freedom. By being ashamed of them, I would be ashamed of America and all it stands for today.

If you understand all this, Friend, you will readily see that I am not unpatriotic when I refer to myself as a Lithuanian and take such pride in things Lithuanian. Instead you will be glad that I have not betrayed my birthright - that glorious Lithuanian heritage of which I am so proud. You will be glad that I speak the beautiful tongue of my forefathers, that I live to hear and sing their songs, that I take a special delight in reading their literature, studying their history, for it helps to make me a better American.

Still more will you be glad that I fight for Lithuanian rights and freedom, for it means that I know the value of freedom and respect the rights of others to pursue life, liberty, and happiness. The enemies of Lithuanian freedom are enemies of American freedom. By fighting them, I fight for America.

Today, when the degradations of Communism menace the freedom of America and the rest of the world, it has become my duty as an American and a Lithuanian to fight for Lithuanian freedom and independence.

Remember these things, Friend, the next time you feel uneasy over my "foreign" leanings and question my patriotism, instead of criticising, join me in the fight for Lithuanian independence. You too are a Lithuanian. By being a better Lithuanian, you will be a better American.

## THE CONSTITUTION OF THE LITHUANIAN ALLIANCE OF AMERICA: "HAVING ASSOCIATED THEMSELVES TOGETHER FOR THE PURPOSE OF CULTIVATING THE SPIRIT OF FRATERNITY AND PRACTICING THE PRINCIPLES OF BENEVOLENCE AND CHARITY"

1956

The Constitution of the Lithuanian Alliance of America, adopted in revised form in 1956, summarized seventy years of experience of the old immigration in an attempt to provide for the social needs of the Lithuanian American and to preserve the culture and heritage of his ancestral homeland.

Name and Language

This association shall be known under the name and title of the LITHUANIAN ALLIANCE OF AMERICA (in the Lithuanian language SUSIVIENIJIMAS LIETUVIU AMERIKOJE), and its offical language shall be the Lithuanian, but the records of the minutes of the meetings of the Supreme Assembly and the Supreme Executive Board, and the books and accounts of the Alliance shall also be in the English language. This organization is not organized for profit and it shall have no capital stock.

Article One; Object

The purpose of this association is:

(a) To unite in fraternal bonds all Lithuanians of good moral character, regardless of sex, creed, faith or political affiliation.

(b) To cultivate the spirit of fraternal brotherhood and to practice the principles of benevolence and charity.

(c) To provide material aid and help to its sick members and also to widows and orphans of deceased members.

(d) To elevate moral, intellectual, social and economic status of its members.

(e) To promote education amongst Lithuanians, by publishing and circulating scientific works, by organizing lectures, by establishing schools, by giving scholarships to its student members and their student children and in various other proper ways.

(f) To issue to adults and juveniles whole life, old age, endowment, whole life combined with old age or endowment, limited payment life, term, disability, annuity, hospitalization, medical, surgical, and dependent benefit certificates and make the specific payments in accordance with the terms of the insurance certificates.

(g) To provide and to maintain a mortuary fund for paying death benefits to the beneficiaries of deceased members, to provide and to maintain a sick benefit fund for aiding its sick members, to provide and to maintain an expense fund for paying expenses of administration, and also to provide and to maintain other funds which might be needed for the promotion of the purposes and objectives of this organization.

(h) To establish and maintain home or homes for its aged members and orphanages for the orphans of its members.

(i) To establish and maintain grounds and buildings of the young and old.

(j) To provide and maintain all funds which might be needed whether in separate or consolidated form.

ARTICLE TWO: Governing Bodies

Convention of the Supreme Assembly and Supreme Executive Board; Supreme Assembly - Its Powers, Composition and Jurisdiction.

Convention

1. The supreme legislative and governing body shall be the Convention of the Supreme Assembly. The Convention of the Supreme Assembly shall be composed of the members of the Supreme Executive Board together with the qualified representatives duly elected by the subordinate lodges.

(a) The business of this organization shall be conducted by a body of seven officers, who shall compose the Supreme Executive Board, and who shall be elected in a manner designated by these By-Laws...

ARTICLE TWENTY-ONE: Laws Governing the Subordinate Lodges and Membership of the Lithuanian Alliance of America

Preamble

For the purpose of effecting uniformity in the administration of the privileges, honors and benefits of the Alliance, the Alliance establishes the following Laws and Regulations for the governing of Subordinate Lodges and District Councils. But Subordinate Lodges and District Councils may make By-Laws for their own guidance not inconsistent with the Constitution and Laws of the Alliance, subject always to the approval of the Supreme Executive Board.

1. The Constitution, the Laws, Rules and usages of the Lithuanian Alliance of America and every article, section and all parts thereto, together with the rituals, requirements of Charter, Benefit Certificates, applications for membership and all blanks used in the Alliance shall be and hereby are made and adopted as part of the law of each and every Subordinate Lodge....

ARTICLE TWENTY-THREE: Lithuanian Alliance of American National Foundation

1. There is established the Lithuanian Alliance of America National Foundation, the corpus of which shall be invested in income producing property and securities, and the income of which shall be invested in income producing property and securities, and the income of which shall be applied from time to time and in such manner as the Trustees of such funds may determine, for the furtherance of such of the charitable, educational, and benevolent activities of the Lithuanian Alliance of America or of its Subordinate Lodges or associations of such Lodges, or otherwise, as the said Trustees may determine; provided, that money or property may be received by the Trustees for other purposes than accumulation in the corpus of the Fund, if the donors thereof so direct and within the general scope of the Foundation....

# THE LITHUANIAN DISPLACED PERSON IN AMERICA

1956

The young journalist Rasa Gustaitis prepared a research paper on the administration of the Refugee Relief Act of 1953. The present was based on the research and personal experiences. Unlike Dr. Cirtautas (infra) she is a representative of the young generation which received its schooling and formed its values abroad, not in the "old country."

Source: Rasa Gustaitis, "The Lithuanian Displaced Person in America," Lituanus, No.1(6), New York, February, 1956, pp. 27-29.

There is no lack of literature about the American immigrant. Theories from many treatises have gained general acceptance, and certain premises are taken for granted. However, new situations prove old theories inadequate and challenge their premises. Therefore, in trying to understand the displaced person in America today, we have to take a fresh look and appreciate the uniqueness of his particular situation. Many people, for instance, take it for granted that the refugee, the immigrant, has come here with the intention of adopting as quickly as possible the customs and the ways of his new country, the United States, and that he is anxious to relinquish his native values and customs. But a person of this opinion is disconcerted when he finds that even when given the opportunity to become assimilated, the D.P. clings to his old culture, does not attempt to become dissolved in the melting-pot, refuses to be integrated. Some of the reasons for this attitude are the same as those which caused old German Quarters and Chinese and Jewish sections to appear in American cities. Others are new.

The D.P.s of the Second World War are refugees from political, religious, and social oppression, as have been many of the previous American immigrants. However, there is an important distinguishing characteristic. The majority of them have come to America as a result of the war which, at the same time that it made them refugees, put their previously free and independent homelands under Soviet domination. Amny of the earlier immigrants came here because of oppression, but it was usually oppression of the particular minority to which they belonged. There is no precedent for the situation of the D.P.'s whose whole countries were overcome by disaster at the time of their emigration. And these countries were intensely conscious of their national aspirations. Many of them had been enjoying political independence only since the First World War.

This is a very important thing to remember in trying to understand the D.P. He does not merely come from the "old country"; he comes from the "enslaved country." He is not homesick only for his friends and relatives overseas; he is also homesick for his nation. This is clearly seen in the literature produced by the Lithuanian D.P.s which is full of longing for Lithuania and deals almost completely with the past and with future hopes rather than with the present. The feeling of national belongingness among exiles is perhaps even more intense than "free home nationalism" was. Therefore, the D.P. feels it a duty to do what is possible to liberate his country and then to rebuild it. Many hope to return to live there after liberation, when it comes. This nationalistic feeling of duty is intensified by the sense of moral duty which always falls upon those who have been lucky in a situation where others were not. Because they got away and others did not, the former have a moral obligation to fulfill. Most D.P.s have lost relatives and friends through Soviet deportation; all have some who still are in Lithuania, and occasionally a letter slips through the censors which gives a glimpse of life in the homeland.

People from countries where nationalism is allowed to express itself and where there is political freedom do not feel the same obligation as do the D.P.s toward their native land. For in Lithuania, there is a drive to make the people lose their national consciousness and become not only physically but also spiritually a part of the Soviet Union. Because there they are not free to protest, because any expression of Lithuanian national consciousness there may lead to death, the job of protesting devolves onto those Lithuanians who are in free countries, i.e., the D.P.s. These things make the D.P.s not merely immigrants but also fighters for a common cause.

National aspirations and the moral sense of duty naturally cause the D.P.s to resist assimilation; in addition, the factors which have in the past caused national cohesion among immigrants are present also. It is a natural human trait to love what is familiar, and for that love to increase when in strange surroundings. The familiar is also secure, and thus national grouping gives security and protection where the new community is hesitant to welcome newcomers or even is hostile to them. It is true that the D.P.s generally found a very warm welcome in the United States. There was general sympathy for their position, as expressed by the D.P. Act passed by Congress in 1948. Although for the past hundred years the traditional Golden Gate of immigration had been closing gradually (the McCarran Act left only a slight crack to squeeze through), and though the sentiment was becoming more and more hostile to further immigrant influx, there was a change for a period of time immediately after World War Two: The United States, one of the few nations not greatly damaged by the war, felt its responsibility towards a ravaged world.

But even with the warmest welcome, their lack of knowledge of the English language, their monetary status, and the fact that they were newcomers limited the opportunities for adjustment in the American community for the D.P.s. Unlike the majority of the earlier American immigrants, many of them are members of the European intelligentsia: educated people, professionals, people familiar with higher culture, specialists. Here they usually find themselves in the cheaper dwelling areas of large cities. The Americans most of them meet are people of lower culture with little education. Very few newcomers can utilize their education in obtaining jobs. Thus, many are forced to leave their skills and professions and do manual labor in the factories. Engineers and scientists generally find that they can use their training in obtaining jobs, but lawyers, former government employees, liberal arts people in general, usually cannot. Thus people from the upper and middle classes of the European countries find themselves forced into a lower-class environment in the United States. They do not find much in common with their neighbors at home and at work, and therefore quite naturally seek fellowship elsewhere among their fellow D.P.s. In the activities of the nationality groups a person can use the talent and ability which is stifled elsewhere. And so the intellectuals write for magazines and newspapers published here in their languages, form the leadership of exile political groups, join clubs of various kinds, express here their need for action. D.P.s not belonging to the intelligentsia also prefer to remain with their national fellows, of course. There is acceptance here - a small, rather compact community where they do not feel strange. Social clubs and athletic groups form. Talent can show itself and be appreciated for the arts are encouraged and supported, and there is opportunity (for those who wish to take it) for participation in various ways. Lithuanian choruses, choirs, and exhibition folk-dancing groups are seen by many American audiences as well as by Lithuanian ones.

A large number of young people seek higher education in the colleges and universities, and among the students, therefore, another section of the national community has developed. Its leaders are generally the older students who had begun their higher education in Germany and Austria and are finishing it here. At this time most of these have already completed their college study, and the younger group is taking over. The students are organized in several student organizations, the most important of which are the Skautai (scouts), the Ateitininkai, a Catholic organization, and the Santara, which attempts to bring together independents of all political and religious opinions. All students are members of the Lithuanian Students' Association, Inc. In cities where a large number of Lithuanian students are found - New York, Boston, Chicago, Detroit, Cleveland and others - these organizations plan activities of a cultural, social, and political nature. Students who find themselves isolated too far from these centers to participate, join in when they can. Conventions, or so-called "study days," are held from time to time, on regional and national bases, and to these the isolated students often come. It is not at all unusual to find someone going from Chicago to Cleveland, from Cleveland to New York, or from Washington to Philadelphia for a weekend convention. It proves an opportunity to exchange ideas and opinions, see old friends, meet new ones. The Lithuanian student travels a great deal, considering his financial status, for that is the only way he can keep some sort of liaison with the other members of the scattered student community. The students are very important because they form the future intelligentsia, the leadership.

And so we see why and how the D.P. communities stay together. The feeling of duty and the sense of mission and loyalty to the group are supported by social pressure, as all mores and morals in all societies are, and the individual is drawn towards the national group by the combination of these various factors. But it is not in vain that American has been called the great melting-pot. Many influences tend to draw these communities apart, inhibit their activities, scatter their members, and slowly force the groups to dissolve.

...There is a tendency to concentrate in the large cities such as New York and Chicago where the largest Lithuanian centers are. One may go to a certain beach on Lake Michigan, for instance, and seem to be in a different country. The restaurants serve "barsciai" and sour milk with steaming boiled potatoes, a tango by Sabaniauskas sounds from the juke-box, and English seems a foreign language there. But such islands are few in number. Many people find themselves in communities where they become separated from their countrymen. The children meet American friends at school, learn American ways, not having the memory of the war and of Lithuania, grow up Americans. Parents try to teach them the language, to instill into them their own interest and feelings. But their efforts are rarely successful and they sadly and hopelessly watch a generation grow up which is very different from their own in its loyalties.

Many students also drift away. They develop interests and ideas which lead them from the nationality group if they find no one within it to share these things with. Occasionally, sitting around a campfire and singing the lovely, melancholy songs of their homeland they feel a longing and a restlessness. But then the current of their lives carries them away from the campfire, and they find this feeling grow weaker.

The nationality group struggles for its existence and the whole struggle is based on one premise that there will be a time to return. Exile politics has little meaning or influence on the international scene, for exile governments have nothing to govern. Their sole purpose now is to serve as a reminder that the status quo in the countries behind the Iron Curtain must not be accepted as satisfactory. And when such reminders are inconvenient to the great powers, they are ignored. Thus the present is looked upon merely as a waiting period: there will come a day when D.P.s will be exiled no more, and, while waiting for this day, the remnant must carry on the life of the nation.

Unfortunately this fight for the survival of the national group can become stifling to individual creativity. For the sake of this sole purpose - the fight for the liberation of his enslaved country and its correlative, the survival of the national group in exile - and the unity necessitated by such purpose, ideas, opinions, and the general outlook of an individual are sometimes greatly affected with respect to these ends-in-view. Associations can become superficial, petty differences loom large, and differences become obscured. Restlessness and unused energy may bring petty splits and disagreements. The phenomenon is not at all unusual among exile groups.

Faced with this situation, some disappointed people decide to break away completely. And so disillusionment, the scattering of the community, lack of a positive goal, and the influence of the American environment are goal under the United States melting pot.

Each Lithuanian then, is caught in the struggle between opposing forces. He is pulled towards the national group and away from it, tossed this way and that. The conflict is most powerful in the case of young people. They are the most susceptible to change, the most flexible, and because of this the pressure of the Lithuanian community is concentrated on them. In the dilemma they may see only this choice: either participate very actively in the group, set the cost perhaps of sacrificing some personal interests or follow those interests at the cost of turning your back upon everything Lithuanian. Marriage is a point which most often forces a decision, and becomes a crossroads for many. The intermarriage of Lithuanians and Americans means almost without exception that the next generation will be completely American. Therefore, a person marrying an American becomes a loss to the Lithuanian nation. To avoid the disapproval of the group and further conflict, such a person often isolates himself from the group and stops participating in its acitivities, especially if he has not been extra-active earlier. The group dwindles.

The problem is great: surely it is the duty of every D.P. to keep reminding the world of his unfortunate countrymen who have no means to speak up. Surely it is his duty to prevent the civilization and culture, of which he is a part, from dying. On the other hand, it is inevitable and not undesirable that he find a permanent place and a home here in the United States, and unrealistic to believe that intermarriage and assimilation can be prevented. What other choice is there? Some Lithuanians, especially educated people, find a third possibility. They find that there need not be a conflict of loyalties. Supporting Lithuanian activity, they also become Americans. Their friends are of both nationalities. These people are then in the position of being able to enrich both the Lithuanian and American cultures by interpreting each to the other, and they have a better chance of avoiding the dangerously narrow parochialism which nationalism often brings with it. The weakness of this alternative lies in the fact, however, that the psychological process of sublimation and integration is quite difficult to achieve.

## REFUGEES: IDEALISTIC AND UTILITARIAN

1957

Dr. K. C. Cirtautas, a refugee himself, wrote a penetrating study of the psychology of Lithuanian displaced persons in his book, The Refugee. The study deals with homelessness as a psychological, social and religious phenomenon. Within his selected frame of reference, the author has done a commendable job of describing and analyzing the refugee.

Source: Excerpt from The Refugee by K. C. Cirtautas. Publisher Meador Publishing Co. of Boston, 1957, pp. 122-127.

After we have scrutinized the outward behavior of the new citizen we can approach him now and ask: what are you thinking about? How do you feel? How do you like being a citizen of a new country? These questions open the areas of his inner life; they will disclose whether the spiritual and cultural values of the new world have also been abosorbed and whether they have enriched his soul. More specifically: Has his mental and emotional life also been assimilated into the new order?

It is not easy for a newcomer to understand the phenomenology and mentality of a new society. It takes much time, keen observations, careful study to come to an appreciation of those practices and processes which differ vastly from the values and responses to which he has been accustome in the old world. Yet, the new citizen feels, almost instinctively and spontaneously, that the new country which admitted him to reside within its borders is wonderful. He can now spend his days in freedom and safety. This realization elicits creative ideas and actions which are simple and good, inspired by the extraordinary events of his shattered life. He proves himself thereby a desirable and useful member of the new society.

The assimilated refugee functions as a person who is motivated by either an idealistic or utilitarian orientation.

What characterizes the idealistic outloo? How does it find expression in daily behaviour? How does the idealist among the assimilated refugees act? What is the nature of his ideal?

Dynamic love for all thos spiritual ideals and values of which he has been deprived and which he regained in the new world is the life blood of his existence. It controls his every thought, the feeling and fibre of his will; he derives nourishment and strength from it. These factors determine his personality. With complete devotion he endeavors to realize those noble ideals in the new country. He becomes a protagonist of true civilization, a champion of genuine humanitarianism, a defender of liberty which is for him the indispensible prerequisite of human existence.

He alone of all men knows by personal experience what liberty really means. He knows its supreme value because he has lived under tyranny. He has personally witnessed the arrest, torture and execution of people for the sole reason that they held different political or social views or worshipped God in another faith; they were made to suffer because they had said or done something which in their conscience they felt to be right and true. He himself had been the victim of the denial of human rights and the suppression of freedom. It is therefore understandable that he lives ardently and gratefully for those ideals which foster true humanity. The ideal of liberty is particularly meaningful to him and he devotes himself passionately to its promotion. He dedicates his life to the cause of freedom.

His missionary efforts begin within his own family circle. He tries to instill the zeal for freedom in his own children; to inspire them with an ardent love of freedom is a sacred task for him. He recognizes no other educational ideal besides education for liberty and the defense of liberty wherever it is suppressed. His children must know that only where life is free is it worth living. Man everywhere must be given the opportunity to think and speak, work and pray in liberty. His children dare never forget that in their father's homeland countless people live in bondage and under terror, anxiously awaiting their liberation. His children must remember day and night that life without freedom becomes diabolical torture. The love of liberty must enter the very blood stream of his children and permeate their whole being. That becomes the supreme educational aim of the idealistic refugee. He lives day and night for that ideal. He uses every opportunity to talk about it, to the neighbor over the fence, to the casual acquaintance on the street, to his fellow workers in shop or office. It is his mission which he never forgets. Whenever the conversation turns to questions of politics, religion, human social orders he raises his voice on behalf of freedom. His children sense it and shall never be able to forget it because their father is so deeply and sincerely concerned about it.

This driving passion for freedom has come about as the result of his personal experiences and his first hand acquaintance with the ideology of totalitarianism. For the native citizen the word freedom rarely means much more than a political or social concept with a positive content. It does not pulsate with life because he has never lived under a dictatorship. He cannot imagine what it means to be unfree, i.e., harrassed, subject to sudden arrest and condemnation to a slow death. The assimilated refugee knows the supreme cruelty of bondage, he has tasted the cup of sadistic terror and learned that freedom is the vital food of the soul, as essential for life as the daily bread. Without it man succumbs slowly and agonizingly. Only the displaced person can appreciate the full blessings of liberty which he is once more privileged to enjoy. Freedom has for him the fragrance of Paradise.

Out of this realization arises the love which characterizes his thoughts and actions. His existence is like an outcry in which the dynamic will for freedom reverberates. His eyes burn like a fire intent to consume the evil of slavery throughout the world.

The reader will now understand why some refugees are so overwhelmed by emotion that they, with tears streaming down their cheeks, falldown and kiss the groun in front of the Statue of Liberty. It is the expression of a profound sense of gratitude, an outward indication of the overwhelming ecstasy of a great love. That is how a human being feels who has at last reached safety.

The idealist among the assimilated refugees is the best qualified teacher of freedom; it has become the most profound verity for him and he vouches for it before the world. In his person alone he awakens and challenges others, reminds them of the fundamental truths of human existence and the need to seek and cherish them anew every day. He is that new citizen who often unconsciously teaches the old citizen. The conviction that liberty under law is a supreme good to be valued and defended unto death, if need be, is the sum and substance of his simple philosophy born out of his own painful experience. It is also the best gift he can proffer the new country in gratitude for the kind reception that has been accorded him.

The utilitarian among the assimilated refugees moves in an entirely different spiritual world. He forms an attachment for the new country, not because his soul is filled with the high hopes of a newly won freedom but because he can now enjoy physical comforts and personal satisfactions. Material comfort constitutes his primary interest. His happiness does not spring from the fact that he can express freely how he feels about matters of political and religious activities, or change his domicile and place of employment as he desires. He pays little attention to these rights because he considers them obvious in a democratic society. He cannot feel particularly enthusiastic about them and discover the source of human happiness in the existence of these rights. What really interests him and satisfies him is the ability to earn enough money to furnish a nice home, eat well, wear attractive clothes, drive a new car, and best of all, put some money in the bank. It does not necessarily mean that he is possessed with the idea of money. An occasional refugee is a miser just as people of other backgrounds are. The materially minded refugee does not desire money for its own sake but for what it can do for him. It can provide for him that comfortable sense of prosperity, of success which sustains and supports his Ego-consciousness. He derives strength from the fact that he and his family are no longer in want for the necessities of life. His gratification over his savings and newly bought property is greater than that of a person who has never experienced poverty and want. That is the real reason why material possessions are so important to him and mean so much for his sense of well-being. They are meant to replace the losses which he has suffered. He can again enjoy in the new home what had been taken from him in the old home, comforts which he had missed so greatly during his long exile. All the opportunities which the new country affords are utilized in an effort to regain and enjoy the amenities of his former existence. By and large he is successful. A proud smile comes over his face when people remark that he has accomplished as much in a few years as others who have lived here all their lives. At the same time, consiously or unconsciously he recognizes his debt to the native citizens. Without their hospitality he would have succumbed in some remote corner of the earth.

When he recalls how difficult it was to achieve success, when he realizes that he now enjoys comforts greater than he ever knew at home, when he thinks of those who still suffer misery and want in the dictator states he must conclude: I have been very fortunate. I must appreciate the new country, I must be loyal to it and help to protect it against harm. Here I am really once more at home: I have a warm room, I can eat nourishing food, I have money to live respectably and with dignity.

Both the idealist and the utilitarian have adjusted themselves to the new standard of living. As their own abilities and tastes direct them, they have embraced the ideals and living habits of the new country. They have become conformists: they have become like Americans or Canadians or Australians as their case may be.

LITHUANIAN AMERICANS APPEAL TO PRESIDENT KENNEDY

TO INCLUDE LITHUANIA IN HIS CONCEPT OF INTERDEPENDENCE

1962

On the occasion of Lithuanian Independence Day, February 16, 1962, a joint delegation of Lithuanian-Americans, representing the leadership of the Lithuanian American Council and the Lithuanian Community Inc. of the United States, were received by President John F. Kennedy in the White House. This was the only occasion for civic leaders of the Lithuanian-American community to meet with President Kennedy. The memorandum quoted below expresses an attempt to integrate the Lithuanian Question in the dynamic President's concept of the interdependency of nations.

Source: Mimeographed Text prepared by the Lithuanian American Council, dated February 16, 1962.

MR. PRESIDENT:

We wish to express our profound gratitude for being received here at the White House on this symbolic date of February 16th which lives in our hearts as the anniversary of the event, 44 years ago, when Lithuania re-emerged as a free and independent state on the principle of national self-determination, restored to her liberty thanks to the political maturity, immense sacrifices and determined spirit of the Lithuanian people.

But this is not a joyful anniversary for us. Twenty-two years after the exhilarating proclamation of the independence of Lithuania, that cherished freedom was struck down. Soviet Red Army divisions overran the country, the free Government of Lithuania was destroyed, and an alien rule of Communist dictatorship was cruelly fastened upon the people.

That tragedy has moved us to come to you, Mr. President, to speak for the oppressed people made silent by the brutal despotism of an alien communist dictatorship. We recall that Lithuania's re-entry to the family of free European States was a historic part of the re-awakening of the wave os self-determination which is still sweeping the globe. In the struggle for Lithuania's freedom, the democratic ideals of political liberty, self-government, and the rights of man played an important part. Lithuania's road toward free statehood was given a vital impetus by President Wilson's inspiring idea of self-determination for all nations. Lithuania's cause is and remains closely tied to the United States of America by common ideals and beliefs.

The delegation expresses the sentiments of millions of our fellow citizens and gives thanks to you, personally, and to your Administration for the adherence to the policy of non-recognition of the Soviet absorption of Lithuania and the other Baltic States. The consistent stand of every Administration of this nation, since July 23, 1940, in refusing to recognize the forced Soviet annexation of Lithuania, Latvia and Estonia, and in extending a continuing recognition to the diplomatic and consular representatives of the Baltic Republics, provides encouragement to the peoples of those small nations that they shall ultimately regain their freedom and their rightful place in the international family of sovereign nations.

While colonies of the Western Nations have been exercising self-determination Lithuania has been transformed into a colonial possession of Soviet Russia. Expropriation, exploitation, pauperization, slave labor, denial of human rights and fundamental freedom, russification, terror, murder, mass deportations - these are the marks of the Soviet occupation in Lithuania, Latvia and Estonia.

With the end of Western colonialism in sight, we believe the time is ripe to hasten the end of Soviet imperialism and colonialism by maintaining a sustained effort, within the United Nations and at other international meetings, for a true test of self-determination and freedom of choice in central and eastern Europe.

We believe that the placing of the U.N. General Assembly's agenda of the problem of the restoration of the sovereignty of Lithuania and other similarly situated nations, in conformance with their peace, non-aggression and friendship treaties concluded with the Soviet Union, would ultimately succeed in arousing world public opinion and in convincing the government and people of the Soviet Union itself that it is in their own interest to abandon colonialism and violations of human rights in favor of the principle of self-determination, respect for treaty obligations and adherence to a world order of law.

At a time when the Russian people are being told of the necessity of undoing the cruel crimes of Stalin, we would ask they be reminded that Lithuania, Latvia and Estonia were among the very first victims of Stalin's aggressive policies, and that their seizure was a direct result of the conspiracy between Hitler and Stalin. Hitler and his criminal regime long ago were condemned by the world at Nuremberg. Stalin has been denounced by the government and ruling party of his own country. And yet the present government of Soviet Russia continues to enjoy the fruits of his crime.

We wholeheartedly support your tenacious efforts to avoid the catastrophe of a nuclear war. We are aware of the difficulties arising out of troubles in various corners of the globe. And we are aware of the heavy burden of responsibility resting on your shoulders. We would not augment them. But we hear the cries of agony and despair of innocent people being unjustly and cruelly wronged. And we believe, even as you have said, that the free nations are not doomed to standing inactive and fighting a rearguard action against Soviet expansionism. There is a vast area for movement between the two extremes of nuclear war and inaction, and we have faith that within that vast area the opportunities will come and will be found to advance the cause of freedom and justice for the peoples of the Baltic States.

We are firmly convinced that in the struggle for world supremacy the forces of freedom and democracy will be victorious. Fully endorsing your determination to "never fear to negotiate," we earnestly ask you, Mr. President, at this momentous juncture of world history to consider the problem of the restoration of Lithuania's independence and freedom as one of the essential prerequisites for the permanent normalization of East-West relations and for the establishment of a just and durable peace in Europe.

We ask further that the people behind the Iron Curtain be told of the concern of the United States for them, and of its sincere desire to assist them in the realization of their aspirations.

We give you our faith and our pledge of readiness of sacrifice to achieve lasting peace with freedom and justice, to help those dear to our hearts, and with a proud feeling of participation in the momentous struggle for a brighter future for all mankind.

# THE UNITED STATES CONGRESS DIRECTS THE PRESIDENT TO RAISE THE BALTIC QUESTION AT THE UNITED NATIONS

1966

House Concurrent Resolution 416 was adopted by the House of Representatives by a record vote of 298 yeas to no nays on June 21, 1965, and unanimously passed by the United States Senate on October 22, 1966.

Calendar No. 1573

89th CONGRESS
2nd Session

H. CON. RES. 416
(Report No. 1606)
IN THE SENATE OF THE UNITED STATES
June 23, 1966
Referred to the Committee on Foreign Relations

September 19 (legislative day, September 7), 1966
Reported by Mr. Fulbright, without amendment
CONCURRENT RESOLUTION

Whereas the subjection of peoples to alien subjugation, domination, and exploitation constitutes a denial of fundamental human rights, is contrary to the Charter of the United Nations, and is an impediment to the promotion of world peace and cooperation; and

Whereas all peoples have the right to self-determination; by virtue of that right they freely determine their political status and freely pursue their economic, social, cultural, and religious development; and

Whereas the Baltic peoples of Estonia, Latvia, and Lithuania have been forcibly deprived of these rights by the Government of the Soviet Union; and

Whereas the Government of the Soviet Union, through a program of deportations and resettlement of peoples, continues in its effort to change the ethnic character of the populations of the Baltic States; and

Whereas it has been the firm and consistent policy of the Government of the United States to support the aspirations of Baltic peoples for self-determination and national independence; and

Whereas there exist many historical, cultural, and family ties between the peoples of the Baltic States and the American people: Be it

Resolved by the House of Representatives (the Senate concurring), That the House of Representatives of the United States urge the President of the United States -

(a) to direct the attention of world opinion at the United Nations and at other appropriate international forums and by such means as he deems appropriate, to the denial of the rights of self-determination for the peoples of Estonia, Latvia, and Lithuania, and

(b) to bring the force of world opinion to bear on behalf of the restoration of these rights to the Baltic peoples.

Passed the House of Representatives June 21, 1965.

Ralph R. Roberts
Clerk

A SUMMIT CONFERENCE OF

LITHUANIAN POLITICAL COMMITTEES IN WASHINGTON, D.C.:

"MANIFESTO ON THE FIFTIETH ANNIVERSARY OF

THE RESTORATION OF LITHUANIAN INDEPENDENCE"

1967

On the eve of the fiftieth anniversary of the Declaration of Lithuanian Independence, the Supreme Committee for Liberation of Lithuania took the initiative in convening a conclave of the authoritative Lithuanian political institutions in the free world. The conclave took place in Washington, D.C., on October 21-22, 1967. A Manifesto was issued reiterating the national aspirations of all Lithuanians, that the age-old Lithuanian nation has an inherent right to exist as an independent country.

Source: Printed Text, published by ELTA.

The Conference to mark the Fiftieth Anniversary of the Restoration of Lithuania's Independence, convened in Washington, D.C., on October twenty-first and twenty-second of the year of Our Lord one-thousand-nine-hundred-and-sixty-seven, in the seven-hundred-and-seventeenth year since the establishment of the Lithuanian Kingdom, and in the fiftieth year since the restoration of Lithuania's Independence announce a Manifesto on the Fiftieth Anniversary of the Restoration of Lithuania's Independence.

The Lithuanian nation, established since ancient times at the Baltic Sea, unified into a Kingdom by King Mindaugas in the year one-thousand-two-hundred-and-fifty-one, for centuries played a significant role in Europe.

The growth of Russian imperialist power led to Moscow's incursion into Lithuania's territories and to the occupation of Lithuania at the end of the eighteenth century. The foreign oppression has not broken down the spirit of the Lithuanian people. The pages of recent Lithuanian history have been filled with the blood and life-sacrifice of insurrectionists, book-smugglers, volunteers and partisans.

In fulfillment of the Lithuanian nation's will to be free and independent, the Council of Lithuania issued the following declaration on February 16, 1918:

- The Council of Lithuania has unanimously decreed at its session of February 16, 1918, to present the following declaration to the governments of Russia, Germany and other states.

- The Council of Lithuania, as the sole representative of the Lithuanian nation, supporting its claims on the recognized principle of self-determination of nations and on the decisions of the Lithuanian National Assembly made at Vilnius on September 17-23, 1917, hereby proclaims the reestablishment of the independent State of Lithuania on a democratic basis with its capital at Vilnius, and announces the separation of that state from all political ties, which previously have linked it with other nations.

Likewise, the Council of Lithuania declares that, in order to fix definitely the foundations of the state of Lithuania and its relations with other states, a Constituent Assembly, elected by the inhabitants in accordance with democratic principles, will be convoked as soon as possible.

The Declaration of February Sixteenth was unanimously confirmed on May 15, 1920, by the freely elected Lithuanian Constituent Assembly. The international community of nations, including Soviet Russia, recognized the restored Lithuanian independence. In its Peace Treaty with Lithuania, signed on July 12, 1920, Soviet Russia stated that it:

--recognized without reservation the sovereign rights and independence of the Lithuanian State, with all the juridical consequences arising from such recognition and voluntarily and for all time abandon all sovereign rights of Russia over the Lithuanian nation and its territory...

The restoration of independent Lithuania and its return to the community of self-governing nations has been the most significant event of the century for the Lithuanian people. The period of independence is a graphic manifestation of the political maturity, economic progressiveness and cultural creativity of the Lithuanian nation.

During the Second World War Lithuania's independence fell victim to a conspiracy between the Soviet Union and Hitler's Germany. The Soviet Union, after having enetered into secret agreements with Hitler's Germany, -- dated August 23 and September 28, 1939, and directed against the independence of Lithuania, Latvia, Estonia, Finland, and Poland, -- occupied Lithuania on June 15, 1940, and by the use of force and perfidy incorporated it into the USSR on August 3, thus violating all the treaties it had signed with Lithuania as well as other international obligations.

THE LITHUANIAN NATION, in commemorating the fiftieth anniversary of the restoration of Lithuania's independence:

Declares to the entire world, be they friends or foes, that it shall never agree with the enslavement of Lithuania, that the Act of February Sixteenth is a sacred and final determination to lead a free and independent life, and that national independence is a condition for the development of national culture and for the very survival of the nation;

Accuses the Soviet Union of the acts of aggression, destruction of Lithuania's independence, genocidal extermination and Russification of the Lithuanian people, colonial exploitation of Lithuania, denial of the basic human rights and freedoms to the Lithuanian people;

Demands that the Soviet Union withdraw its army, police, and administration from Lithuania;

Asks the governments and parliaments of the free world to use all their means to restore the independence of Lithuania;

Appeals to the United Nations for action to liquidate the Soviet aggression against Lithuania and to the conscience of mankind to support Lithuanian efforts to restore their independence.

LITHUANIANS LIVING IN FREEDOM, respectful and proud of the determination of their nation to resist the occupying power; bowing their heads before those who fell in the fight for freedom; paying honors to the patriarchs of the National Awakening and to the signatories of the Declaration of February; dutybound and favored by the liberty that surrounds them to speak and act on behalf of their unfree nation; are united in their effort to free Lithuania from Soviet occupation, and therefore declare the year one-thousand-nine hundred-sixty-eight - the fiftieth year since the restoration of Lithuania's independence - the Year of Lithuania's Fight For Freedom.

Although Lithuania's struggle for liberty has been going on since the very first days of the Soviet occupation, the Year of Lithuania's Fight for Freedom should activate in a new and special way the forces of all free Lithuanians in their effort to restore the power of the Declaration of February Sixteenth. The united forces of the Lithuanian nation against Soviet Russian occupation will again make the Declaration of February Sixteenth a living reality.

Liberation of nations is advancing inexorably from west and east, south and north. The oppression of Russian bolshevism will not be able to prevent Lithuania's liberation, the living goal of the entire nation.

In the progress march of mankind, freedom is more powerful than oppression.

Long live free and independent Lithuania!

Washington, D.C.
October 22, 1967

THE DIPLOMATIC SERVICE OF THE LITHUANIAN REPUBLIC:
Min. Stasys Lozoraitis
Chief of Lithuanian Diplomats

COMMITTEE FOR A FREE LITHUANIA:
Min. Vaclovas Sidzikauskas
Chairman

THE SUPREME COMMITTEE FOR LIBERATION OF LITHUANIA:
Dr. J. K. Valiunas
President

LITHUANIAN COMMUNITY OF THE UNITED STATES:
Bronius Nainys
Chairman

LITHUANIAN AMERICAN COUNCIL:
Antanas Rudis
Chairman

LITHUANIAN COMMUNITY OF CANADA:
Antanas Rinkunas
Chairman

THE WORLD LITHUANIAN COMMUNITY:
Juozas Bachunas
Chairman

AMERICAN STATESMEN SUPPORT LITHUANIA'S RIGHT

TO NATIONAL INDEPENDENCE

1968

The government of the United States was and still is the staunch advocate of the policy of nonrecognition of the incorporation of Lithuania into the Soviet Union. The legation of the Republic of Lithuania still functions with full accreditation to the United States Government. The Lithuanian consular offices still perform their duties in several major cities. Every year, since the early 1940s, on the occasion of Lithuanian Independence Day, February 16, members of the United States Congress have spoken out on Lithuania's behalf on the floor; their remarks have been recorded in the Congressional Record. Special statements or messages have been issued regarding Lithuania's legal status by the secretaries of state, from George Marshall to Henry Kissinger.

Source: V. Salnas, Tragedy of Lithuania and Other Baltic Countries, Philadelphia, Committee to Commemorate the 50th Anniversary of Independence to Lithuania, 1968, pp. 28-36.

The nonrecognition of Soviet aggression against the Baltic States became an integral part of the United States foreign policy by all past Administrations. In defense of that policy, Mr. John F. Dulles has said:[1]

> Some may say that it is unrealistic and impractical not to recognize the enforced incorporation of Estonia, Latvia, and Lithuania into the Soviet Union. We believe, however, that a despotism of the Soviet type cannot indefinitely perpetuate its rule over hundreds of millions of people who love God, who love country, and who have a sense of personal dignity.

On numerous occasions, statesmen, political leaders and people believing in justice, have made and still make statements contrary to the Soviet propaganda that Lithuania became one of the Soviet states legitimately and by her own volition....President Dwight D.

---

1. Hearings before the Select Committee to Investigate the Incorporation of the Baltic States into the USSR, House of Representatives, 83rd Congress, 1st Session, Washington, U.S.G.P.O., 1954, p.4.

Eisenhower pointed out the Soviet aggression in these words:[2]

> The Soviet Union, in violation of solemn treaty agreements, seized control of the Baltic Republics of Estonia, Latvia and Lithuania, and then, after having illegally incorporated these countries into the Soviet Union, proceeded to deport and liquidate great numbers of their citizens. These wrongs of aggression and terror have left a profound impression on the American people. It is reflected in our steadfast policy of continuing to recognize the diplomatic representatives of the independent Baltic States and in our cherished hope that these countries shall again live in freedom.

Speaking of all European nations which have been deprived of their freedom, President John F. Kennedy said:[3]

> All of us...must be faithful to our conviction that peace in Europe can never be complete until everywhere in Europe men can choose, in peace and freedom, how their countries shall be governed.

...on the occasion of the 41st anniversary of the Declaration of Baltic Independence, Secretary of State John F. Dulles stated:[4]

> In June 1940 the Soviets demanded that the Governments of the three Baltic states be reorganized, demands which the Baltic states were powerless to resist...There followed rigged elections which resulted, in July of 1940, in the incorporation of the Baltic states, as Soviet Socialist Republics, into the Soviet Union...Today, over 18 years later, we wish to assure the people of Lithuanian, Latvia, and Estonia once more that they are not forgotten. The United States still aspires, in the words of the Atlantic Charter, to see sovereign rights and self-government restored to those who have been forcibly deprived of them.

George W. Ball, Acting Secretary of State wrote to Mr. J. Kajeckas, Charge d'Affaires of Lithuania in Washington on February 7, 1965:[5]

> Nearly 25 years have elapsed since the sovereign Lithuanian nation lost its national independence in the wake of the illegal annexation by the Soviet Union. But the indomitable spirit of the Lithuanian people and their yearning to live in freedom and independence have not been dimmed throughout these years....The United States thereby not only accords recognition to the Lithuanian people's devotion to the cause

2. Americans for Congressional Action to Free the Baltic States, Illinois Divison, The Baltic States, Chicago, 1967.
3. Ibid.
4. U.S. Department of State Bulletin, March 2, 1959, Vol. 40, p. 299.
5. Congressional Record, February 16, 1965, p. 2.

> of freedom and national independence, but expresses its confidence that this cause will ultimately prevail.

On December 6, 1967, the Vice-President of the United States Hubert H. Humphrey conveyed the best wishes of President Lyndon B. Johnson to the delegation of the American Lithuanian Council visiting the White House. Among other things, Mr. Humphrey said:[6]

> As you know, the United States government has consistently refused to recognize the forcible incorporation of Lithuania by the Soviet Union and has continued to support the cause of self-determination for all the Baltic peoples. The courage and the dedication with which the Lithuanian people both at home and abroad have maintained their national identity in the face of great adversity is an inspiration to free men everywhere...You know that the principle of self-determination applies universally.

In his rebuke of Anatoli Kuznetsov's attacks upon the United States actions in Vietnam, U.S. Ambassador A. J. Goldberg stated in the General Assembly of the United Nations on November 28, 1967:[7]

> In the past generation or so, the Soviet Union has been perhaps the world's leading advocate of defining aggression... Now let us see how this great definer of aggression has conducted itself in practice during the same generation - testing it by its own definitions offered to the United Nations. In 1933 the Soviet Union incorporated its proposed definition of aggression into non-aggression treaties with Estonia, Lithuania and Latvia. Seven years later these states were forcibly occupied and incorporated into the Soviet Union...

6. "Humphrey - The United States Supports Baltic Self-Determination," ELTA, No. 1 (113), January 20, 1968, New York, p. 3.
7. *Ibid.*, p. 4.

## CONTEMPORARY LITHUANIAN LANGUAGE SCHOOLS: REPORT TO THE SECOND SESSION OF THE SEVENTH COUNCIL OF THE LITHUANIAN COMMUNITY, INC. OF THE U.S.A. 1974

The preservation of the mother tongue and conveyance of cultural traditions among the young are an effective guarantee that an ethnic minority will retain its consciousness for another generation. During the last twenty years, the Lithuanian Community Inc. Lietuviu Bendruomene, transformed the various Lithuanian language Saturday Schools into a systematic educational system with grades and study norms. These part-time schools came to be called Lithuanistic Schools (Lithuanistics is the multi-discipline study of Lithuanian language, history, culture, and geography). The following report, delivered by Stasys Rudys, chairman of the Council on Education (Svietimo Taryba), during the June 15, 1974 session of the Lithuanian Community Council in Chicago, reflects on the current status of community-based Lithuanian language instruction.

1. The Number of Schools and Pupils.

The Council on Education received statistical information from 35 Lithuanistic Schools for the 1973-74 school year. The following institutions offer daily instruction: the Montesori Children's Home in Chicago and four Lithuanistic schools: St. Mary's in Marquette Park (Chicago), Immaculate Conception in Brighton Park (Chicago), St. Anthony's in Cicero, Ill. and St. Casimir's in Los Angeles, Cal. Lithuanian is taught in Brockton, Mass. on Fridays. The Grand Rapids, Mich. school is open on Sundays. Two schools function on both Saturdays and Sundays, namely, the Lithuanian Evangelical Lutheran Teviskes Parochial School and the Philadelphia Lithuanian high school. The other 26 Lithuanistic schools offer their courses on Saturdays.

There are 21 primary-level schools with 8 grades. Eight schools offer a partial or complete high school course in Lithuanian. Four high schools operate with courses running from the firth through the twelfth grades.

Currently there are 16 kindergartens. Nine schools offer special classes for students who know little Lithuanian. The Los Angeles Saturday School offers a teaching course with ten students enrolled in the pedagogical program. Of special note is the Pedagogical Lithuanistic Institute of Chicago. Forty-eight students attend its classes. In addition, the Institute offers a correspondence course to 44 subscribers.

According to our statistical data, during this school year, the total enrollment in the Lithuanistic schools is 2,129 pupils and students. This figure does not include the students attending the Kristijonas Donelaitis' School in Chicago, and the Ausra Lithuanistic School of Detroit. We did not receive any reports from these two schools. Last year 408 students attended the Donelaitis' School, and 17 were enrolled in the Detroit School. Therefore, if enrollments have not changed, then the total number of children enrolled in Lithuanian language schools is 2,554...

For the record, the 35 schools have a faculty of three hundred and fifteen teachers (218 women and 97 men).

2. Teaching Methods and Reading Matter.

We now have primers and exercise manuals for all of the grades of instruction in the Lithuanistic school system. Our present concern is to provide them with new and improved publications. To be sure, in changing the literature and history programs of the higher schools, new primers and textbooks must be prepared and printed. Thus, for example, Vincentas Liulevicius' text for the 9th grade, "The History of the Lithuanian Nation and State" was recently published. A second volume has been prepared for the press. If we succeed in giving this manuscrip to the printer during the summer, the tenth grade students will be able to use the book next year. New textbooks on Lithuanian literature are being prepared. We must try to find an author quickly for a primer to be used by children who are not fluent in Lithuanian or who do not have any knowledge of the language. Unfortunately, to date no one has undertaken the writing of such a primer. Our search for authors must continue.

During the summer months we will publish a text on Lithuanian geography for the 3rd and 6th grades. A geography exercise book for the 8th grade is in preparation. The following books, prepared by the former members of the Council on Education, have been given to the press: Rev. J. Gutauskas' Krikscionybe Lietuvoje (Christianity in Lithuania), Stasys Barzdukas' Lietuvis savo tautoje, valstybeje, bendruomeneje (The Lithuanian in His Nation, State, Community), Prof. A. Klimas and S. Barzdukas' A Lithuanian Language Dictionary for School and Home, and Richard Scarry's Best Word Book Ever in a Lithuanian edition. Last autumn Juozas Andrius' "Map of Lithuania" was printed.

The Juvenile Reading Matter Contest was a success; three books suitable for young people have appeared off the press: Mrs. D. Bindokis' Parkas anapus gatves (The Park Across the Street), J. Svabas-Gylys' Gabriuko uzrasai (Gabby's Notes), and N. Jankus-Uzubalis' Nuo 9 iki 1 (From Nine To One). Vladas Vijeikis' Saigunas will appear soon. In addition, a collection of children's poetry, J. Mingela's Kiskio pyragai (The Rabbit's Cakes) was recently published. We have a number of juvenile books in preparation, but their printing entails great financial difficulties and delays. We believe that this year's Youth Reading Matter Contest will not be any less successful than the last one.

3. Financing.

The Council on Education operates on funds obtained from the Lithuanian Foundation (Lietuviu Fondas), the Executive Board of the Lithuanian Community Inc., and from the sale of the school books. The following funds were obtained for the 1973-74 School Year: $24,000.00 from the Lithuanian Foundation, $887.00 from the Executive Board of the Lithuanian Community, and $9,000.00 from publications sold.

4. The Training of Teaching Personnel

Under our working conditions, the training of teachers is a most difficult problem. The best conditions are in Chicago, because the Pedagogical Lithuanistic Institute functions there. The other communities have tried to set up Lithuanian studies courses or pedagogic classes in the higher schools. Such courses are offered in only one school this year.

Our young teachers gain skills by working in the schools, especially where experienced principals or directors are able to assist or to guide them. Study weeks are organized and offered for young instructors. We also publish a magazine, Svietimo Gaires (The Guidelines of Education).

5. Lithuanistic Studies in the Universities.

Dr. Janina Reklaitis taught three Lithuanian language courses at the Chicago Circle of the University of Illinois. Forty-four students attended the courses. The University officials are pleased with the number of enrolled students and with the work of Dr. Reklaitis. Our Council on Education was instrumental in setting up the courses. Financial assistance was obtained from the Lithuanian Foundation. During the Spring Semester the Lithuanian language was also taught at the University of Michigan, Ann Arbor campus. This course received a grant from the University itself. Fifteen students enrolled in this course. It is thanks to the students' initiative that this course was established. The lecturer was Mrs. Lilija Grazulis. Financial assistance will have to be obtained from the Lithuanian Foundation in order to continue the language program at the University of Michigan.

## LITHUANIAN AMERICANS IN THE AMERICAN MAINSTREAM

## 1974

The point scarcely needs to be made that the older generations of Lithuanian immigrants helped to build the industrial might of America by working in the coal fields, by laying track, by sweating in the steel mills and foundries, and by butchering livestock in the Chicago yards. Their sons and cousins who came over after the Second World War have pioneered in electronics and petrochemical synthetics. Many gadgets and processes are the brainchildren of meticulous Lithuanian-American scientists.

If a Lithuanian Who's Who were ever compiled it would contain the names of several thousand men and women of science. The Lithuanian American scientist is active in his field of specialization. Lithuanian names and surnames can be found in scientific journals. Thus, for example, Martin Ycas Jr. is active on the editorial board of the Journal of Theoretical Biology. A random review will disclose that in 1974 Lithuanian-Americans took active roles in various scholarly conferences. During the conference of geophysicists in Washington, the following Lithuanians presented papers: Arvydas Kliore, Vytautas Klemas, Richard Legeckas and Vytenis Vasyliunas. Mrs. A. Vygantas, V. Uzgiris and E. Uzgiris read papers at a conference of biochemists and biophysicists in Minneapolis. A number of prominent scientists attended international meetings and conferences, they included Jonas Bilenas, and Raymond Viskanta in Japan, Arvydas Kliore in Brazil, Antanas Butkus and Vytenis Vasyliunas in Italy, V. Damusis, and J. A. Rackauskas in Switzerland. Algirdas Avizienis gave a computer science seminar at the University of Vilnius in Lithuania.

The following Lithuanian Americans have earned doctorates and have gained national recognition for their contributions in various fields:

Chemistry: Walter Abromaitis heads agricultural chemical research at Armour Industrial Chemical Co. Vytautas Adomaitis conducts water chemical experiments for the U.S. Fish and Wild Life Service. Jurgis Anysas teaches quantum chemistry at DePaul University. Petras Avizonis works with optical lazers and studies the interaction of high intensity energy with matter for the United States Air Force Weapons Laboratory. Edward Alfred Bartkus manages advanced technological systems development for IBM. Edward Peter Bartkus supervises ne information service developments for Du Pont De Nemours. Rimgaudas Budrys works on structural rearrangements in high polymers. Antanas Butkus analyses disorders of lipid metabolism and arteriosclerosis at the Cleveland Clinic Foundation. Dow Chemical Co. employs James M. Gaidis in silicon and organometallic chemistry. Henry Leo Jankauskas is polymer research chemist at Du Pont De Nemours. Vytautas Zachary Jankus studies neutron thermalization at the Argonne National Laboratory. Bruno Jaselskis teaches analytical chemistry at Loyola University.

Arnold Francis Kaulakis manages the cryoplants labe of Standard Oil. Arvydas Kudirka works with the Atomic Energy Commission on thermodynamics and hydrodynamics. Joseph Laukonis works on oxidation reduction catalysts for General Motors Corp. Arthur Peter Malinauskas is a member of the research staff of Oak Ridge National Laboratory; he conducts experiments on thermal transpiration and the transport properties of gases.

Other distinguished Lithuanian American scientists engaged in research in polymers, analytical, organic, organometallic and physical chemistry include: Edward Matulevicius, Raymond Matulis, Joseph Paukstelis, George Paulik, Frank E. Paulik, George Paulikas, Edward John Pavilanis, Alexander A. Petrauskas, Albin G. Pinkus, Joseph Raksys, Ruta Rakutis, Saulius Simoliunas, John Anthony Skarulis, Victor Snieckus, David Joseph Stanonis, Raymond J. Suplinskas, Juozas Rimvydas Vaisnys, Joseph K. Valaitis, Edmun Vasiliauskas, Joseph Vebra, Raymond Viskanta, Phillip Anthony Waitkus, Henry Yuska, Richard Zdanis, Danute Zukas and Eugene Zytkus.

Electrical Engineering: Algirdas Avizienis works for the Jet Propulsion Lab of the California Institute of Technology; his specialty is fault-tolerant and self-repairing digital systems. Vytautas Klemas conducts lazer research and satellite experiments for General Electric. Arvydas J. Kliore conducts experiments to measure planetary atmospheres and radio propagations for the Jet Propulsion Lab of the California Institute of Technology.

Biological Sciences: Lithuanian scholars are well represented in the biological and medical sciences: John Vytautas Burba (pharmocologist), Bernard Gerulat (immunochemist), Algirdas Greichus (parasitologist), Yvonne Greichus (zoologist), David Francis Grial (forest ecologist), Edward F. Jankus (physiologist), John Edward Klimas Jr. (physiologist), Marilyn Kvetkas (microbiologist), Kazys Labanauskas (horticulturist), Victor Matukas (dental pathologist), Daniel Matulionis (embryologist), Raymond Oslapas (endocrinologist), Felix Paulbinskas (biophysicist), Gerald J. Paulik (fishery biologist), Vytautas Pavilanis (virologist), Birute Pleskys-Jakstas (parasitologist), Bronius Povilaitis (plant geneticist), Joseph Rachis (biochemist), Rozalija Somkaite(pharmaceutical analyst), Peter Steponkus (cryobiologist), Robert Joseph Sydiskis (eriologist), Casimir Tumasonis (entomologist), Vainutis Vaitkevicius (oncologist), Zigfridas Vaituzis (microbiologist), Eleanor Ruth Witkus (biologist), Albert Yurkstas (dental prosthetician), and Alex Griganauzas (pharmocologist).

Mathematics: Ceslovas Masaitis works on numerical analysis at the Ballistics Research Lab at the Aberdeen Proving Grounds. Victor R. Staknis teaches mathematical topology at Northeastern University. A specialist in astrophysics, Romuald Zalubas works on thorium wavelength standards for the National Bureau of Standards in Washington, D.C.

Other Technologies: Edward Butkewicz is a systems engineer with the Naval Aircraft Weapons Center. Paul Mazeika is employed by the United States Naval Oceanographic Office as an oceanographer. Well versed in atmospheric physics, Vincent J. Stakutis is a senior technical staff member of the United States Air Force and conducts experiments in satellite reconnaissance systems and nuclear weapon environment effects. The Illinois Institute of Technology employs Sarunas Uzgiris in mechanical systems design and stress analysis. The metallurgist Eugene G. Zukas analyses the properties of heavy metal composites for the Los Alamos Science Laboratory. Pranas Zunde is an internationally-known systems engineering consultant, specializing in the design of information and communications systems.

Lithuanians have also established themselves in the social and behavioral sciences. Professor Vytautas Bieliauskas specializes in psychotherapy and has chaired numerous conferences of physiologists and psychologists. Vytautas Kavolis has written extensively on the sociology of art and social pathology.

Lithuanian American singers have performed with the Metropolitan Opera of New York. The first singer to be admitted to the Met was Anna Kaska (Ona Katkauskaite). In 1927 this lyric contralto from Hartford made her debut with the Lithuanian State Opera in Kaunas. After studying voice in Milan, Miss Kaska was invited to sing with the Metropolitan Opera in 1936. She performed with the Met until 1946. Polyna Stoska (Apolonija Stoskute) first performed at the Met with the Russian Opera Society in 1936. During World War II this lyric dramatic soprano sang with USO concerts. She made her debut with the Met in 1947.

The baritone Algird Brazis joined the Metropolitan Concert Co. in 1939 and performed in major cities. He also performed with the Mid West Opera Co., the Chicago American Opera Co., and the Theatre of the Air Program. In 1951 Algirdas Brazis was invited to join the Metropolitan Opera where he sang starring roles for four years. The lyric bass-baritone Arnold Voketaitis began his singing career while serving in the United States Army. He appeared on the Soldier Parade on Station ABC. In 1958 Mr. Voketaitis was invited as a soloist by the New York City Center Opera. After successful appearances on radio and television Mr. Voketaitis was invited to sing with the Met in 1965. The lyric soprano Lilian Shukis is the latest Lithuanian soloist at the Met. Miss Shukis made her debut in the MacMillan Theatre of Toronto in 1964. In 1966 she joined the New York Metropolitan Opera. After a success star performance in Munich, Germany, in 1969, Miss Shukis was given starring roles with the Metropolitan Opera.

Antanas Smetona Jr. is an accomplished concert pianist.

Lithuanians have entered the motion picture industry. The late Laurence Harvey (Laurynas Skinkis) was born in Lithuania. The following motion picture and television actors are of Lithuanian descent: Charles Bronson (Casimir Businskis), Kaz Garas (Kazys Gaizutis), Ann Jillian (Jurate Nauseda), Ruta Lee (Ruta Kilmonis), Ruth Roman (Romanauskas), Jacque Sernas, and Joanna Shimkus.

The Mekas Brothers - Jonas and Adolfas - are acknowledged leaders of the underground and avantgarde film movement. Their films "Guns of the Trees" (1961), "The Brig" (1964), "Halleluyah The Hills" (1963), "Double-Barrelled Detective Story" (1965), and "Windflowers" (1967) are avantgarde classics. Jonas Mekas is the film critic editor of the Village Voice in New York. He also writes idyllic and free form poetry in Lithuanian.

Between 1952 and 1961 Algis Budrys established a reputation as a first rate science fiction writer, publishing over 200 short stories and novelettes. He has written a number of science fiction novels and has contributed to such magazines as *Esquire* and the *Saturday Evening Post*. Algis Budrys is managing editor of his own science fiction publishing house in Chicago.

As in the past, Lithuanians have excelled in sports. They are represented by Johnny Podres in baseball; Catcavage, Dick Butkus, and Johnny Unitas in football. A rising star is the nineteen-year-old tennis champion Vitas Gerulaitis....

# APPENDIX I

## THE LITHUANIAN AMERICAN POPULATION

## DURING THE PERIOD OF THE GREAT IMMIGRATION,

## 1899-1914

How many Lithuanians came to this country during the great waves of immigration? Lithuanian writers estimate that before 1899, some 275,000 Lithuanian immigrants arrived in the United States. The Lithuanian demographer gives a more realistic figure of one third that number. Relatively accurate statistics are obtainable after 1899 when the United States Government established a separate Lithuanian classification. The practice of grouping the Lithuanians in the Slavic Division was followed prior to that year. Even the figures for 1899-1914 are only relatively accurate because many Lithuanians were listed by immigration officials as Poles, Russians, or Germans. Furthermore, there is no record of children born to the arrivals in the United States.

V. K. Rackauskas compiled detailed statistical tables for the years 1899 through 1914. These statistics were based on United States Immigration Service Reports and census figures. Mr. Rackauskas published his tables in the book Amerika arba Rinkinys Ivairiu Faktu (New York, 1915). The statistics were later reprinted in the Lithuanian Alliance almanac, SLA Kalendorius, 1918 (New York, 1918). Several of his tables are reproduced below in translation.

Table #1. Lithuanian Immigrants to the United States

| Year | Men | Women | Totals |
|---|---|---|---|
| 1899 | 5,291 | 1,567 | 6,858 |
| 1900 | 7,683 | 2,628 | 10,311 |
| 1901 | 6,499 | 2,316 | 8,815 |
| 1902 | 8,576 | 3,053 | 11,629 |
| 1903 | 10,721 | 3,711 | 14,432 |
| 1904 | 8,854 | 3,926 | 12,780 |
| 1905 | 13,842 | 4,762 | 18,604 |
| 1906 | 9,429 | 4,828 | 14,257 |
| 1907 | 18,716 | 7,168 | 25,884 |
| 1908 | 8,522 | 5,198 | 13,720 |
| 1909 | 10,284 | 4,970 | 15,254 |
| 1910 | 15,360 | 7,354 | 22,714 |
| 1911 | 10,473 | 6,554 | 17,027 |
| 1912 | 8,098 | 5,980 | 14,078 |
| 1913 | 16,069 | 8,578 | 24,647 |
| 1914 | 12,282 | 9,302 | 21,584 |
| Total | 170,699 | 81,895 | 252,594 |

Table #2. Lithuanian Immigrants By Age

| Year | 0-14 Years | 14-45 Years | Over 45 Years |
|---|---|---|---|
| 1899 | 448 | 6,276 | 134 |
| 1900 | 790 | 9,347 | 174 |
| 1901 | 712 | 7,986 | 117 |
| 1902 | 949 | 10,479 | 201 |
| 1903 | 1,137 | 13,078 | 217 |
| 1904 | 1,317 | 11,279 | 184 |
| 1905 | 1,474 | 16,875 | 255 |
| 1906 | 1,270 | 12,765 | 222 |
| 1907 | 1,563 | 23,928 | 393 |
| 1908 | 1,256 | 12,173 | 291 |
| 1909 | 1,088 | 13,694 | 472 |
| 1910 | 1,813 | 20,381 | 520 |
| 1911 | 1,382 | 15,331 | 314 |
| 1912 | 1,186 | 12,635 | 257 |
| 1913 | 1,760 | 22,438 | 449 |
| 1914 | 2,040 | 19,059 | 485 |
| Total | 20,185 | 227,724 | 4,705 |

Table #3. The Immigrants and Their Travel Sponsors

| Year | Self-Paid Fares | Paid By Relatives | Paid By Others |
|---|---|---|---|
| 1908 | 7,967 | 5,639 | 114 |
| 1909 | 10,692 | 4,460 | 102 |
| 1910 | 14,004 | 8,538 | 172 |
| 1911 | 9,259 | 7,688 | 80 |
| 1912 | 7,221 | 6,784 | 73 |
| 1913 | 13,833 | 10,681 | 133 |
| 1914 | 9,182 | 12,259 | 143 |
| Totals | 72,158 | 56,049 | 817 |

Table #4. States Wherein the Lithuanians Settled, 1899-1914.

| State | No. of Lithuanians | State | No. of Lithuanians |
|---|---|---|---|
| Alabama | 13 | District of Col | 8 |
| Alaska | 16 | Florida | 138 |
| Arkansas | 14 | Georgia | 9 |
| Arizona | 14 | Hawaii | 3 |
| California | 232 | Idaho | 9 |
| Colorado | 280 | Illinois | 47,339 |
| Connecticut | 15,952 | Indiana | 1,996 |
| Delaware | 17 | Indian Territory | 105 |

| State | No. of Lithuanians | State | No. of Lithuanians |
|---|---|---|---|
| Iowa | 973 | North Carolina | 11 |
| Kansas | 109 | North Dakota | 118 |
| Kentucky | 20 | Ohio | 4,841 |
| Louisiana | 15 | Oklahoma | 162 |
| Maine | 2,234 | Oregon | 125 |
| Maryland | 3,896 | Pennsylvania | 70,019 |
| Massachusetts | 37,049 | Rhode Island | 861 |
| Michigan | 3,427 | South Carolina | 6 |
| Minnesota | 387 | South Dakota | 44 |
| Mississippi | 52 | Tennessee | 15 |
| Missouri | 901 | Texas | 54 |
| Montana | 50 | Utah | 17 |
| Nebraska | 315 | Vermont | 530 |
| Nevada | 2 | Virginia | 147 |
| New Hampshire | 2,023 | Washington | 574 |
| New Jersey | 12,656 | West Virginia | 2,014 |
| New Mexico | 9 | Wisconsin | 4,045 |
| New York | 37,912 | Wyoming | 21 |
| | | Total | 252,594 |

Table #5. Lithuanian Immigrants by Professions

1909-1914

Professionals:

| | | | |
|---|---|---|---|
| Lawyers | 5 | Writers | 18 |
| Actors | 2 | Teachers | 37 |
| Architects | 10 | Musicians | 61 |
| Doctors | 6 | Editors | 4 |
| Electrotechnicians | 12 | Sculptors & Painters | 8 |
| Engineers | 18 | Other professions | 32 |
| Clergy | 37 | Total | 255 |

Craftsmen:

| | | | |
|---|---|---|---|
| Stonecutters | 29 | Millers | 59 |
| Brewers | 11 | Machinists | 114 |
| Miners | 3,160 | Mechanics | 112 |
| Textile workers | 42 | Woodworkers | 28 |
| Weavers | 70 | Metalworkers | 32 |
| Goldsmiths | 10 | Butchers | 86 |
| Saddlers | 49 | Dressmakers | 11 |
| Barbers | 49 | Masons | 276 |
| Cigar-makers | 2 | Stokers | 60 |
| Carpenters | 1,845 | Wheelwrights | 26 |
| Gardeners | 60 | Sewers | 2,285 |
| Tanners | 44 | Garment workers | 542 |
| Pattern-cutters | 2 | Women Garment Workers | 320 |

| | |
|---|---|
| Photographers................13 | Tinsmiths.....................51 |
| Iron-workers................455 | Printers......................27 |
| Sailors.....................156 | Cabinet makers...............143 |
| Furriers......................8 | Locksmiths...................546 |
| Blacksmiths.................707 | Plumbers......................10 |
| Bakers......................150 | Tobacco-pickers...............10 |
| Hatters......................25 | Tobacco curists................4 |
| Clerks......................244 | Upholsterers...................9 |
| Bookbinders..................17 | Painters.....................132 |
| Shoe-makers.................775 | Plasterers.....................2 |
| Watchmakers..................32 | Other artisans...............223 |
| Shipwrights...................3 | Total.....................13,185 |
| Locomotive Engineers.........78 | |

Other Occupations:

| | |
|---|---|
| Agents........................3 | Farmers......................593 |
| Bankers.......................1 | Farm Laborers.............79,059 |
| Laborers.................71,485 | Teamsters.....................20 |
| Manufacturers................12 | Fishermen......................6 |
| Merchants...................174 | Others.......................241 |
| Saloonkeepers.................4 | Non-laborers (women & children included)....45,672 |
| Servants and Manuals.....41,884 | Total....................239.177 |
| | Grand Total..............252,594 |

## APPENDIX II

### LITHUANIAN AMERICAN POPULATION BY STATES: 1960

(Source: United States Census of Population 1960)

<u>New England</u>:

| | |
|---|---|
| Maine | 1,800 |
| New Hampshire | 1,934 |
| Vermont | 224 |
| Massachusetts | 40,921 |
| Rhode Island | 1,780 |
| Connecticut | |

<u>Middle Atlantic</u>:

| | |
|---|---|
| New York | 55,652 |
| Pennsylvania | 58,092 |

<u>East North Central</u>:

| | |
|---|---|
| Ohio | 17,641 |
| Indiana | 5,126 |
| Illinois | 75,034 |
| Michigan | 21,236 |
| Wisconsin | 7,442 |

<u>West North Central</u>:

| | |
|---|---|
| Minnesota | 3,105 |
| Iowa | 1,488 |
| Missouri | 2,650 |
| North Dakota | 151 |
| South Dakota | 161 |
| Nebraska | 1,794 |
| Kansas | 460 |

<u>South Atlantic</u>:

| | |
|---|---|
| Delaware | 526 |
| Maryland | 9,962 |
| Dist. of Col. | 1,462 |
| Virginia | 2,368 |
| W. Virginia | 1,057 |
| North Carolina | 605 |
| South Carolina | 272 |
| Georgia | 751 |
| Florida | 6,606 |

<u>East South Central</u>:

| | |
|---|---|
| Kentucky | 590 |
| Tennessee | 428 |
| Alabama | 390 |
| Mississippi | 178 |

<u>West South Central</u>:

| | |
|---|---|
| Arkansas | 218 |
| Louisiana | 367 |
| Oklahoma | 474 |
| Texas | 2,177 |

<u>Mountain</u>:

| | |
|---|---|
| Montana | 273 |
| Idaho | 96 |
| Wyoming | 102 |
| Colorado | 899 |
| New Mexico | 342 |
| Arizona | 1,314 |
| Utah | 156 |
| Nevada | 250 |

<u>Pacific</u>:

| | |
|---|---|
| Washington | 1,708 |
| Oregon | 854 |
| California | 19,421 |
| Alaska | 167 |
| Hawaii | 143 |
| Total | 402,846 |

| | |
|---|---|
| Percentage of Total Population | 1.2% |
| Urban Dwellers | 359,433 |
| Town Dwellers | 37,919 |
| Rural Population | 5,494 |

N.B. Federal Census figures have always underestimated the Lithuanian American population. In 1960, total Lithuanian stock refers to the country of origin and includes first and second generations. The foreign born Lithuanian population is based on the mother tongue of the respondents, and the second generation (natives with one or both parents Lithuanians) is usually determined by subtracting the foreign born from the total figure. The fallacy in Federal Ethnic Statistics lies in the fact that they do not take into consideration persons beyond the second generation.

# APPENDIX III

## LITHUANIAN AMERICAN PUBLICATIONS

### Lithuanian American Daily Newspapers

Draugas, 4545 W. 63rd Street, Chicago, Illinois 60629. Pp. 8 daily; 14 pp., Saturday. Annual subscription: $23.00.

Naujienos, 1739 Halsted Street, Chicago, Illinois 60608. Pp. 6 daily. Annual subscription: $15.00.

### Twice Weekly Newspapers

Dirva, 6907 Superior Avenue, Cleveland, Ohio 44103. Pp. 8. Annual subscription: $13.00.

### Weekly Newspapers

Darbininkas, 341 Highland Boulevard, Brooklyn, New York 11207. Pp. 12. Annual Subscription: $10.00.

Keleivis, 636 Broadway, South Boston, Massachusetts 02127. Pp. 6. Annual subscription: $7.00.

Sandara, 940 West 33rd Street, Chicago, Illinois 60608. Pp. 8. Annual subscription: $4.00.

### Biweekly Newspapers

Laisvoji Lietuva, 2618 West 71st Street, Chicago, Illinois 60629. Pp. 12. Annual subscription: $6.00

Tevyne, 307 West 30th Street, New York, New York 10001. Pp. 8. (Tabloid). Annual subscription: $4.00.

Vienybe, 192 Highland Boulevard, Brooklyn, New York 11207. Pp. 12. (Tabloid). Annual subscription: $7.00.

### Monthly Newspapers

Akiraciai, 62-21 So. Maplewood, Chicago, Illinois 60629. Pp. 16. Annual subscription: $6.00.

Garsas, 71-73 So. Washington Street, P.O. Box 32, Wilkes Barre, Pennsylvania 18703. Pp. 8. Annual subscription: $4.00

Lietuviai Amerikos Vakaruose, 4364 Sunset Boulevard, Hollywood, California 90029. Pp. 8. (Tabloid). Annual subscription: $3.00.

Academic Journals in English

Lituanus, P.O. Box 9318 Chicago, Illinois 60690. Pp. 80 quarterly. Annual subscription: $8.00.

Aidai, 341 Highland Boulevard, Brooklyn, New York 11207, Pp. 48 monthly. Annual subscription: $12.00.

Ateitis, 6641 So. Albany Avenue, Chicago, Illinois 60629. Pp. 32 monthly. Annual subscription: $5.00.

Gaudeamus, c/o R. Petrauskas, 190 Bruce, Windsor, Ontario, Canada. (Mimeographed newsletter).

I Laisve, 7034 Hartcrest Drive, Rancho Palos Verdes, California 90724. Pp. 80 quarterly. Annual subscription: $7.00

Karys, 341 Highland Boulevard, Brooklyn, New York 11207. Pp. 40 Monthly. Annual subscription: $9.00.

Laiskai Lietuviams, 2345 W. 56th Street, Chicago, Illinois 60636. Pp. 34. Monthly. Annual subscription: $5.00.

Laivas, 4545 W. 63rd Street, Chicago, Illinois 60629.

Lietuviu Dienos, 4364 Sunset Boulevard, Hollywood, California 90029. Pp. 24 Monthly (Lithuanian and English). Annual subscription: $12.00.

The Marian, 4545 W. 63rd Street, Chicago, Illinois 60629. Pp. 40 Monthly (English). Annual subscription: $6.00.

Metmenys, c/o Dr. V. Kavolis, Dickinson College, Carlisle, Pennsylvania. Pp. 176. Irregular. Annual subscription: $7.00.

Musu Vytis, 5747 So. Campbell Avenue, Chicago, Illinois 60629. Pp. 32 Monthly. Annual subscription: $5.00.

Naujoji Viltis, 7150 So. Spaulding Avenue, Chicago, Illinois 60629. Pp. 120. Irregular. Annual subscription: $3.00.

Seja, 1649 N. Broadway, Melrose Park, Illinois 60160. Pp. 72 Monthly. Annual subscription: $5.00.

Skautu Aidas, 7418 So. Claremont Avenue, Chicago, Illinois 60636. Pp. 32 Monthly.

Sv. Pranciskaus Varpelis, 341 Highland Boulevard, Brooklyn, New York 11207. Pp. 32 Monthly. Annual subscription: $3.00

Tevynes Sargas, 220 North 7th Street, Mount Vernon, New York 10550, Pp. 224. Irregular. Annual subscription: $5.00.

Varpas, 1214 N. 16th Avenue, Melrose Park, Illinois 60160. Pp. 166. Annual. Annual subscription: $3.00.

Vytis, 1467 Force Drive, Mountainside, New Jersey 07092. Pp. 24 Monthly. Annual subscription: $5.00.

Specialized Publications

Eglute, Immaculate Conception Convent, Putnam, Connecticut 06260. (Children's magazine) Pp. 32 Monthly. Annual subscription: $5.00.

Medicina, 10326 Kipling Street, Westchester, Illinois 60153. (Physician's journal). Pp. 32. Annual subscription: $10.00.

Muzikos Zinios, 341 Highland Boulevard, Brooklyn, New York 11207. (Church Organists and Musicians journal) monthly.

Technikos Zodis, 5025 So. Rockwell Street, Chicago, Illinois 60029. (Journal for Engineers, Chemists and Architects).

# APPENDIX IV

## LITHUANIAN AMERICAN CULTURAL INSTITUTIONS

### Foundations and Research Centers

Association for the Advancement of Baltic Studies, Inc., Allentown, Pennsylvania.

The Cultural Council of the Lithuanian American Community, Inc., Chicago, Illinois.

Institute for Lithuanian Studies, Chicago, Illinois.

Lithuanian Foundation (*Lietuviu Fondas*), Chicago, Illinois.

The Lithuanian Independence Fund, Richmond Hill, New York.

Lithuanian Research Institute, Inc., New York City.

Lithuanian Roman Catholic Academy of Sciences, Putnam, Connecticut.

National Foundation of the Lithuanian Alliance of America, New York.

Toward Freedom (I Laisve) Fund, Brooklyn, New York

### Archives and Museums

American Lithuanian Cultural Archives, ALKA, Putnam, Connecticut.

Professor Juozas Zilevicius Library of Lithuanian Musicology, Jesuit Youth Center, Chicago, Illinois.

Stanley Balzekas Museum of Lithuanian Culture, Chicago, Illinois.

World Lithuanian Archives, Jesuit Youth Center, Chicago, Illinois.

### Lithuanian Cultural Societies and Clubs

Algimantas Mackus Cultural Fund, Chicago, Illinois.

American Lithuanian Child Care Association (ALVUD), Chicago, Illinois.

Boston Lithuanian Cultural Club, Boston, Massachusetts.

Educational Council of the Lithuanian American Community, Inc., Chicago, Illinois.

Lithuanian Catholic Press Society, Chicago, Illinois.

Lithuanian Folk Dance Institute of the Lithuanian American Community, Inc., Chicago, Illinois.

Lithuanian Historical Society, Chicago, Illinois.

Lithuanian Jurists Association, New York City.

Lithuanian Writers Association, Chicago, Illinois.

Lituanus Foundation, Inc., Chicago, Illinois.

Pedagogical Lithuanistic Institute, Chicago, Illinois.

The Saturday Night Cultural Club of Boston, Boston, Massachusetts.

Tevynes Myletoju Draugija or Association of Lithuanian Patriots, Chicago, Illinois.

The Vaizgantas Cultural Club, Brooklyn, New York.

# APPENDIX V

## MAJOR LITHUANIAN INSTITUTIONS IN AMERICA

### REPUBLIC OF LITHUANIA:

The Legation of the Republic of Lithuania
The Honorable Juozas Kajeckas, Charge d'Affaires
2622 16th Street, N.W.
Washington, D.C. 20009

Consulate General of the Republic of Lithuania in New York
The Honorable Anicetas Simutis, Consul General
41 West 82nd Street
New York, New York 10024

Consulate General of the Republic of Lithuania in Chicago
The Honorable Josephine Dauzvardis, Honorary Consul General
6147 South Artesian Avenue
Chicago, Illinois 60629

### POLITICAL AND CIVIC NATIONAL ORGANIZATIONS:

The Supreme Committee for Liberation of Lithuania
Dr. Kestutis J. Valiunas, President
29 West 57th Street
New York, New York 10019

The Committee for a Free Lithuania
Vytautas Vaitiekunas, Chairman
29 West 57th Street
New York, New York 10019

The Lithuanian American Council
The Executive Board
Dr. Kazys Bobelis, Chairman
2606 So. Maplewood Avenue
Chicago, Illinois 60629

The Lithuanian World Community, Inc.
The Executive Board
Bronius Nainys, President
6804 So. Maplewood Avenue
Chicago, Illinois 60629

The Lithuanian American Community of the USA, Inc.
National Executive Committee
Juozas Gaila, President
121 Antietam Road
Cherry Hill, New Jersey 08034

The United Lithuanian Relief Fund of America
The National Executive Board
Mrs. Marija Rudis, Chairman
2606 West 63rd Street
Chicago, Illinois 60629

## BIBLIOGRAPHY: BOOKS IN ENGLISH

Augius, Paulius, ed., Lithuanian Art in Exile, Munich, 1948.

Baltrusaitis, Jurgis, Lithuanian Folk Art, Munich, 1948.

Balys, Jonas, Lithuania and Lithuanians, A Selected Bibliography,

______________, Lithuanian Narrative Folksongs, Washington, DC., 1954.

Baravykas, V., English-Lithuanian Dictionary, Vilnius, 1958.

Beliajus, Vytautas F., The Dance of Lietuva, Chicago, 1951.

Budrys, Stasys, Paprockas, Vaclovas, Dr. Alexander Carolus Cursius-Curtius, Chicago, 1967.

Burton, Katherine, Lily and Sword and Crown, The History of the Congregation of the Sisters of St. Casimir, Milwaukee, Wisconsin, 1958.

Chase, Thomas, The Story of Lithuania, New York, 1946.

Cirtautas, Kazimieras C., The Refugee, A Psychological Study, Boston, 1957.

Dambriunas, L., Klimas, A., Schmalstieg, W.R., Introduction to Modern Lithuanian, New York, 1966.

Gaida, Pranas, ed., Lithuanians in Canada, Toronto, 1967.

Gerutis, Albertas, ed., Lithuania, 700 Years, New York, 1969.

Haiman, Miecislaus, Polish Past in America, 1608-1865, Chicago, 1939.

Harrison, E.J., Lithuania's Fight for Freedom, New York 1952.

Herlitas, J.A., English-Lithuanian Dictionary, Klaipeda, 1931.

Jurgela, Constantine R., History of the Lithuanian Nation, New York, 1948.

Kaslas, Bronis J., The USSR-German Aggression Against Lithuania, New York, 1973.

Kemesis, Feliksas, Cooperation Among Lithuanians in the United States of America, N.L. 1924.

Kucas, Antanas, St. George's Parish, Shenandoah, Pa., Brooklyn, 1968.

Lalis, Antanas, Lithuanian-English and English-Lithuanian Dictionary, Chicago, Third Edition, 1915.

Lavinskas, Frank, The Lithuanian Press in USA from 1879 to 1955, Long Island City, New York, 1956.

Lithuanian Business Directory, Chicago, 1932.

Lithuanian Chamber of Commerce of Illinois, Chicagos Vadovas-Chicago Guide, Chicago, 1952.

Margeris, Algirdas, The Lithuanian Americans and a Dictionary of English Loanwords in Lithuanian, 1872-1949, Chicago, 1956.

Norem, Owen J., Timeless Lithuania, Cleveland, 1943.

Palmer, V.M., Field Studies in Sociology, Chicago, University of Chicago, 1928.

Park, Robert E., The Immigrant Press and Its Control, New York, 1922.

Peteraitis, Vilius, Lithuanian-English Dictionary, Noerdling, 1948; Second Edition, Chicago, 1960.

Pewtress, Harry, Marlborough's English-Lithuanian and Lithuanian-English Dictionary, London, 1939.

Roberts, Peter, The Anthracite Coal Communities, New York, 1904.

Roucek, Joseph, American Lithuanians, New York, 1939.

Rubulis, Aleksis, Baltic Literature, Notre Dame, Indiana, 1970.

Rugsenas, Algis, Day of Shame, New York, 1973.

Senn, Alfred E., The Emergence of Modern Lithuania, New York, 1959.

Sienkiewicz, Henry, Portrait of America, (Translated by Charles Morley) New York, 1959.

Simutis, Anicetas, ed., Lithuanian World Directory, New York, Second Edition, 1958.

Sirvaitis, C.P., Religious Folkways in Lithuania and Their Conservation among the Lithuanian Immigrants in the United States, 1952.

Tarulis, Albert N., American-Baltic Relations, 1918-1922, Washington, 1965.

Vaiciulaitis, Antanas, Outline History of Lithuanian Literature, Chicago, 1942.

Vardys, V.S., Lithuania under the Soviets, Portrait of a Nation, 1940-1965, New York, 1965.

Variakojyte-Inkeniene, Marlborough's Lithuanian Self-Taught, London, 1958.

Vitkauskas, Arejas, An Immigrant's Story, New York, 1956.

Wolkovich, William L., From the Nemunas to the Assabeth, A History of the Lithuanians of Hudson, Mass., Hudson, 1966.

Encyclopedias

Lithuanian Encyclopedia Press, Encyclopedia Lituanica, Vols. I-III, Voston, 1971-1974.

Fiction

Andriekus, Leonardas, Amens in Amber, New York, 1968.

Baranauskas, Antanas, The Forest of Anyksciai, (Translated by Nadas Rastenis), Los Angeles, 1956.

Baronas, Aloyzas, Footbridges and Abysses, New York, 1965.

Beliajus, Vytautas F., The Evening Song - A Selection of Lithuanian Folk Tales, Legends and Fables, San Diego, 1954.

Donelaitis, Kristijonas, The Seasons, (Translated by Nadas Rastenis), Los Angeles, 1967.

Gliauda, Jurgis, House upon the Sand, New York, 1963.

______________, The Sonata of Icarus, New York, 1968.

Katzenelenbogen, Uriah, The Daina, An Anthology of Lithuanian and Latvian Folk Songs, Chicago, 1935.

Kreve, Vincas, The Temptation, New York, 1965.

Kudirka, Vincas, Memoirs of a Lithuanian Bridge, New York, 1961.

Landsbergis, Algirdas, Mills, Clark, ed., The Green Linden, Selected Lithuanian Folktales, New York, 1964.

Ramonas, Vincas, Crosses, Los Angeles, 1954.

Sinclair, Upton, The Jungle, (Numerous editions).

Seinius, Ignas, Rejuvenation of Siegfried Immerselbe, New York, 1965.

Vaiciulaitis, Antanas, Noon at a Country Inn, New York, 1965.

Zobarskas, Stepas, Lithuanian Folk Tales, New York, 1959.

______________, Lithuanian Quartet, New York, 1959.

______________, Selected Lithuanian Short Stories, New York, 1963.

Historical, Political and Social Monographs
on Lithuania and Lithuanians

Audenas, Juozas, Twenty Years' Struggle for Freedom of Lithuanian, New York, 1963.

Backus, Oswald, Motives for West Russian Nobles in Deserting Lithuania for Moscow, Lawrence, Kansas, 1957.

Benedictsen, Age Meyer, Lithuania the Awakening of a Nation, Copenhagen, 1924.

Budreckis, Algirdas, Soviet Occupation and Annexation of the Republic of Lithuania, New York, 1968.

Budreckis, Algirdas, The Lithuanian National Revolt of 1941, Boston, 1968.

Cantons, Albert, Saint Casimir, Boston, 1958.

Gimbutas, Marija, Ancient Symbolism in Lithuanian Folk Art, Philadelphia, 1958.

Gimbutas, Marija, The Balts, New York, 1963.

Harrison, Ernest J., Lithuania, 1928, London, 1928.

Hordynski, Joseph, History of the Late Polish Revolution and the Events of the Campaign in Lithuania, Boston, 1833.

Jurgela, Constantine, Gecys, Kazys, Suziedelis, Simas, Lithuania in a Twin Teutonic Clutch, New York, 1945.

Klimas, Petras, Ghillebert de Lannoy in Medieval Lithuania, New York, 1945.

Koncius, Juozas, Vytautas the Great, Grand Duke of Lithuania, Miami, 1964.

Lithuanian-American Catholic Services, The Chronicle of the Catholic Church in Lithuania, 1975.

Lithuanian American Community, Inc., The Violations of Human Rights in Soviet Occupied Lithuania, A Report for 1971, 1972, 1973, 1974, Glenside, Pennsylvania, 1972-1975.

Lithuanian Information Bureau, The Lithuanian-Polish Dispute, London 1923.

Maciuika, Benedict V., Lithuania in the Last 30 Years, New Haven, 1955.

Manning, Clarence, The Forgotten Republics, New York, 1952.

Page, Stanley W., The Formation of the Baltic States, Cambridge, Massachusetts, 1959.

Pakstas, Kazys, Lithuania and World War II, Chicago, 1947.

Pakstas, Kazys, The Lithuanian Situation, Chicago, 1941.

Pelekis, K., Genocide, Lithuania's Threefold Tragedy, Venta, 1949.

Petruitis, Jonas, Lithuania under the Sickle and Hammer, Cleveland,

Pick, F.W., The Baltic Nations, London, 1945.

Royal Institute of International Affairs, The Baltic States, London, 1938.

Sacks, Abraham A., An Excursion to Lithuania, New York, 1934.

Sapoka, Adolfas, Lithuania Through the Ages, Munich, 1948.

Sapoka, Adolfas, Vilnius in the Life of Lithuania, Toronto, 1962.

Savasis, J., The War Against God in Lithuania, New York, 1966.

Select Report No. 14, Communist Takeover and Occupation of Lithuania, Washington, D.C., 1955.

Senn, Alfred E., The Great Powers, Lithuania and the Vilnius Question, 1920-1928, Leiden, 1966.

Simutis, Anicetas, Economic Reconstruction of Lithuania after 1918, New York, 1942.

Sliupas, Jonas, Lithuania in Retrospect and Prospect, New York, 1915.

Stukas, Jack J., Awakening Lithuania, Madison, N.J., 1966.

Supreme Committee for Liberation of Lithuania, Living in Freedom, Augsburg, 1949.

Tarulis, Albert, Soviet Policy Toward the Baltic States, South Bend, Indiana, 1959.

Tauras, K.V., Guerrilla Warfare on the Amber Coast, New York, 1962.

Tautvaisa, Halina, The Cemetery of Nations in the Siberian Tundra, London, 1968.

Swettenham, John A., The Tragedy of the Baltic States, London, 1952.

Trakiskis, A., The Situation of the Church and Religious Practices in Occupied Lithuania, New York, 1944.

Vaitiekunas, Vytautas, A Survey of Developments in Captive Lithuania, Surveys for 1962, 1963-64, New York, 1963, 1965.

Vaitiekunas, Vytautas, Lithuania, New York, 1965.

Valiukas, Leonard, Lithuania, Land of Heroes, Hollywood, California, 1962.

Zadeikis, Povilas, Introducing Lithuania, New York, 1930.